THE DOUBLE DUTCHMAN

In November 1943, the Big Three conference at Teheran produced a plan to win Hungary from her German allegiance, to the side of the Allies. New Zealand private, Roy Natusch, newly escaped from Germany to Hungary, and posing as a Captain, was soon part of the plot . . .

His wartime career was unique by any standards. From Castles to prison cells; from Hungarian police to the Gestapo . . . his incredible escapes defied the laws of probability. A man with the audacity to impersonate a Dutch officer – without knowing a single word of Dutch – and convince his German interrogators that he was genuine!

This exciting book is one of the most unusual escape stories to come out of the last war . . .

Francis S. Jones

The Double Dutchman

CORGI BOOKS
A DIVISION OF TRANSWORLD PUBLISHERS LTD

THE DOUBLE DUTCHMAN

A CORGI BOOK 0 552 10764 6

Originally published in Great Britain by
Robert Hale Ltd.

PRINTING HISTORY
Robert Hale edition published 1977
Corgi edition published 1978

This book is set in Intertype Baskerville

Corgi Books are published by
Transworld Publishers Ltd.,
Century House, 61–63 Uxbridge Road,
Ealing, London W5 5SA

Made and printed in Great Britain by
Cox & Wyman Ltd., London, Reading and Fakenham

CONTENTS

To NEUBRANDENBERG
BERLIN STETTIN
BRESLAU
R. Danube
VIENNA
CZECHOSLOVAKIA
BRATISLAVA
CAMP 17A
HEGYESHALOM
WEINER NEUSTADT
Lake
Neusiedler
KOMOROM
AUSTRIA
BUDAPEST
SZOMBATHELY
HUNGARY
R. Mur
GAAS
Lake
Balaton
WOLFSBERG
RADKERSBURG
WINDISCHE BUHELN
MARBURG
POSRUK HILLS
ST. LORENZEN
BACHER HILLS
R. Drava
FIESTRITZ
CILLI
MOTTNIG
KAPOSVAR
SZULOK
SZIGETVAR
LITTAI
LJUBLJANA
YUGOSLAVIA
BARC
SIKLOS
R. Gurr
R. Sava
SEISENBERG
Zagreb
0
50
TOPLITZ
MOTTLING
TSCHERNOMBL
R. Kulpa
Miles
SEMIC

CHAPTER ONE

THE BLACK MARE

THE grey mare shivered uneasily in her stall as Natusch came nearer. She turned her head over her shoulder as far as she could, tried unsuccessfully to focus him with her sound eye, and relaxed instantly as he realized his mistake and moved quickly to the correct side. The New Zealander frowned in self-reproach as he made reassuring noises to the nervous animal.

He went closer, caressed the mare's flank, and felt a familiar nausea begin to rise as she nuzzled him, her right eye now confident and trusting, the pupil in her left eye black and dilated and unseeing. Natusch spoke soothingly to her, rubbed her flank again – no one ever touched the head of this animal – smiled at the little ripples of pleasure that flowed along her body, and for the hundredth time cursed Obergefreiter Wilhelm Rueger.

The eye was Rueger's doing. Before he left his farmstead, Obergefreiter Rueger, now standing duty as a Wehrmacht corporal somewhere on the Eastern front, had tethered his mare securely, had sterilized and heated a needle, and had plunged it into the centre of her left eye with considerable skill and with complete callousness.

The German knew precisely what he was doing. He was blinding the mare, deliberately mutilating her, and only one reason compelled such obscene butchery. It was a basic one that to his way of thinking didn't brook argument. Herr Rueger loved his wife more than he did his horse.

He drove the needle in far enough to destroy the pupil, but not sufficiently deep to collapse the structure of the eye itself. It was a dreadful parody of a technique which he knew at first hand was sometimes used by veterinary surgeons to cure cataracts: it was also a highly skilled operation which brought untold agony to the unfortunate mare, made her an instant discard from requisitioning Army zealots, and almost, but not quite, spoilt her sweet nature.

Natusch felt his spasm subside as quickly as it had arisen. Maybe, he reflected, the German corporal wasn't a sadist after all, despite this powerful indication to the contrary. He would value his horse – both his horses – and possibly even love them as only a true farmer can. One thing was certain. He would want at all costs to keep the grey mare from the Wehrmacht's clutches; but there was only one way he could do it, only one way to ensure that she'd still be at Gaas when, God willing, he would be allowed to shed his field-grey uniform and get back to things that mattered. Herr Rueger may well have stood aghast at the measure he proposed to take. What he knew beyond any shadow of doubt was that it would be infallible.

There was also the other, the more powerful consideration which was forcing him into such appalling barbarity. Without the grey mare, as the corporal realized only too well, his toil-worn wife, whom he loved dearly, would never be able to keep the farm going.

There had been no need to maim the second horse. The Obergefreiter had many worries, more now perhaps than he'd had before, but the black mare hadn't contributed to them. She had, as Rueger was well aware, an inbuilt and invincible defence against any marauding quartermaster, or come to that, he had reflected, against any other thief. She was a superb animal, could work all day and all night if necessary, could see with both eyes, and could kick at lightning speed with all four feet. She accepted no one's authority except that of her owner and his wife. She humoured them, and worked willingly for them because she chose to, and for no other reason; but no one else could approach within yards of her. If they did, it was at their peril. The black mare, as Rueger and his wife suspected, and as everyone else in the neighbourhood knew for certain, was possessed of the Devil. She was in no danger of being requisitioned.

The Wehrmacht had her on their list, of course, as was to be expected, and when her turn came, they didn't dally. That much, Frau Rueger decided grimly, as she reread the Army's curt letter, was also predictable, but she didn't lose heart. The grey mare, at least, was now safe from them. The other horse, the black one, might yet decide to have its own say in what went on.

The Wehrmacht official, an overbearing man from Weiner Neustadt, arrived at the farm complete with horse-van, two bridles and a receipt book a week after the Obergefreiter had departed. He located the Frau, flourished his requisitioning authority, and spoke briefly. He didn't bother to introduce himself, nor to offer any word of comfort or condolence at the departure of the farm's owner, still less at the proposed seizure of his two horses. 'Zwei Pferden, bitte,' was all he deigned to say. His tone was brusque and domineering, full of the aggressiveness that is so often the hallmark of a successful *embusqué,* and the obligatory 'please' did nothing to diminish its unpleasantness. A poker-faced Frau Rueger pointed out the stable to him, and the Heeresgebeit representative, no longer acknowledging her, walked over and entered it. The Frau waited, unsmiling as ever, but with an anticipatory gleam in her eye that should have warned the official.

He emerged from the stable about a minute later, dishevelled, his face grey with fright, and made a hasty and undignified retreat from the farm. He went back at speed to Weiner Neustadt. From there, word passed down the line, and the message registered: and since that initial and abortive attempt to conscript the black mare into the Fuehrer's service, no other government agent had yet approached the farm. It no doubt brightened the distant Obergefreiter's day when his wife's carefully phrased letter retailed the occasion to him.

Natusch finished rubbing down the grey mare, allowed her to nuzzle him once again, and then moved over towards her younger companion. He was careful here, and watched intently as she, too, submitted to the daily grooming. A few minutes later, he gave her sleek flanks their last caress of the handbrush, smoothed them with the flat of his hand, and, still on his guard, left the now docile killer horse and began brushing out the stable. He worked steadily, a half-smile gradually appearing on his face as he recalled the treatment that both the mare and Frau Rueger had been meting out to him only a fortnight before.

Unexpectedly, the harassed Frau had found herself worse off than her neighbours, despite her husband's foresight.

Very few of these peasant farmers had any horses at all, either because they'd never been able to afford draught animals, or because the Wehrmacht had successfully commandeered them. Frau Rueger still had two – the best for miles around – but the second part of the Obergefreiter's plan had misfired. She could approach the mares, even if no one else could, and she could do the harnessing and the stable work well enough on her own, but she soon discovered that she and her husband had overlooked a vital point in their planning.

She found she couldn't use her horses. Herr Rueger had never had need to entrust them to anyone other than himself, and consequently, his wife had yet to hold the reins in her hands. She took them up confidently enough, but a shock awaited her. After one abortive attempt with the heavy mowing machine, she had to admit to herself that she had neither the strength nor the agility to work the two animals together. It was a man's job, heavy, laborious work, and she was nowhere near strong enough.

One horse, by itself, was of little use. The mowing machine, the big farm cart, the plough, and most of the other implements were tandem-drawn, and as there was no one else who could go near them, the two mares had been more or less idle since the day Herr Rueger had kissed his wife goodbye and set off on his long journey. Instead of being out in the fields, where they were wanted, badly wanted now that the harvest was looming up, they had remained for the most part in their stable, doing nothing, eating their heads off, a liability instead of the asset that they should have been, and something of a nightmare – the black horse especially – to every forced worker and to every prisoner-of-war who had so far arrived at the farm.

At first, Natusch didn't realize what was upsetting his new employer. He was greeted with the same look of instant disapproval which she had given all his predecessors, but for the first few days he was engaged in menial tasks that didn't take him near the stable. Frau Rueger didn't mention the horses either, but the New Zealander learnt from her quickly enough that no one had yet stayed here long, and that most of the rejected workers had been sent back in disgrace to the Stalag. The Frau's tone was flat and hostile, and her disclosure alarmed Natusch.

It alarmed Dai Davies even more. Back at the lager, the big Welsh sergeant listened attentively as the New Zealander retailed the day's events, his frown growing deeper as the story unfolded.

'You'll have to find out what's biting her, Roy,' he said at length. He spoke urgently. 'Whatever it is, fix it. We've got to stay here another month. If you get sent back to the Stalag, we're finished.' Dai's brow wrinkled. 'But she's only just met you,' he protested. 'She doesn't know what you can do yet. What's she want to carry on like that for?' He looked up suddenly. 'She's not a sex-maniac, is she?' he hazarded.

Natusch shuddered at the thought. 'No,' he said fervently. 'Anything but, thank God. But something's wrong. The chap before me – I think he was a Pole – only lasted a week. I've no idea why. Maybe I'll find out tomorrow. I'll do my best anyway. I can't do more.'

The New Zealander did his best to succeed where the others before him had so mysteriously failed; but it wasn't easy. He worked hard and willingly, but his gaunt German employer soon showed she was in no mood to give praise. Frau Rueger had a lot to put up with, and she quickly transferred a growing hatred of the recalcitrant black mare and its half-blind stablemate to her newly-arrived *Kriegsgefangener* helper, and as had happened before, hate fed on its own flame. Within days she was openly hostile to Natusch. He found that he could do nothing right, grew alarmed when his farm rations suddenly decreased, and felt panic touch him when his employer stopped the meagre wine issue altogether.

The black mare, paradoxically, saved Natusch. He had had no warning about her, and on his sixth day with the irascible German woman he went into the stable, unhitched the mare's bridle rope and walked her clear of the stall. Maybe, he decided, if he were to do an extra stint here and clean out the place, the Frau might relent a little. It was worth trying.

The black mare allowed herself to be led out into the cobbled yard without protest. The unsuspecting New Zealander left her there, and was picking up a fork and shovel when the mare, puzzled perhaps at the temerity of this rash invader, finally made up her mind and came at him with teeth bared and ears flat. Natusch spotted her from the corner of his eye and dived under the heavy wagon in the nick of time.

He remained under the wagon. He stayed there for quite a time, motionless, watching the black horse intently, trying to analyse her behaviour, and awakening, as her ferocity increased, to the reason both for Frau Rueger's malcontent and for the rapid exodus of workers from her farm.

The mare, robbed of her advantage, occupied most of his thoughts. She seemed to go suddenly berserk, and she began prancing and stamping around the heavy cart, her nostrils dilated, her breath a series of rapid snorts, a mask of froth beginning to form at her muzzle. Every now and again she turned and lashed out with her hind feet. Her fury grew with each kick, but her wits didn't leave her. Natusch noted that she attacked the wagon body only at its centre, just above the place where he was sheltering. She seemed to be stalking him, and to be applying an intelligence to her task that was more human than equine.

He stayed where he was, lying prone and inert. The thought occurred to him that this rampaging animal might be insane, but he dismissed it. He knew horses, knew them better than most men, and had he been more alert, the black mare's demeanour would have warned him that something was wrong.

His knowledge of horses had been hard-gained. The advent of war had found Natusch – the odd surname came from a long-dead Polish forbear – studying architecture at Wellington, which was a far cry from his home in the rugged countryside above Hawkes Bay. He had been born and bred on a farm there, and had found, whilst still in his early 'teens, that his *métier* lay in horses generally, and in horse-breaking in particular. There wasn't, he had once boasted in youthful arrogance, anything on four legs in the North Island that he, Roy Spencer Natusch, couldn't ride, and there had been a grain of truth in the boast. He had been thrown out of many a saddle, but he was a competent horseman for all that, the more so because somehow he seldom failed, eventually, to establish an accord with even the wildest animal.

Horses do go mad, he remembered, as he lay under the wagon, just the same as people, although less frequently. He had never seen a demented one, but he knew that their affliction followed a set pattern, and the mare, despite her paroxysm, wasn't displaying any of the classic symptoms of equine insanity. No, he decided, she wasn't off her head, but he couldn't recall having seen such sustained wickedness as this before.

He had encountered some horses that were bad enough in all conscience. The worst, undoubtedly, had been a half-wild stallion which had tried to throw him, then to savage him, and, failing in both, had galloped straight over the edge of a low cliff. He had abandoned saddle at the last moment, and somehow the sweating animal had managed to land without breaking its legs. He had remounted as it struggled to its feet, and had found the brute still full of fire. Natusch pursed his lips as the mare finally gave up her assault and went back into the stable. Compared with her, even that determined home-bred stallion seemed placid.

He wouldn't have gone near the mare again, for all his experience, if events hadn't forced his hand. A letter arrived from the distant Obergefreiter, spoke of mud and privation, and hinted at defeat – even in the parts that weren't blue-pencilled – and immediately Natusch's relations with the grieving Frau Rueger went from bad to worse. It became clear that only a few more days would elapse before he, too, would be back at the Stalag.

He accepted the challenge. He gave it a good deal of thought because he knew full well that this mare could easily kill him, and would do so given the chance, and he rejected some ideas which were plainly impracticable. In the end, he settled for a club that was heavy, rounded at one end, and nearly two feet long. Even then, he didn't fancy the odds, but again, he had no option. It seemed the only way to offer any chance at all of meeting the present crisis successfully.

Next morning he waited until Frau Rueger was away from the farm before going to the stable. There was no one about. He swung the door open, jumped back a pace or two, and almost immediately the unfettered black mare charged through the doorway. Natusch, anticipating her action, measured her for a split second and then struck with all the force he could muster.

The blow was harder than he had intended. It caught the mare flush on her forehead, and by rights should have killed her, but she seemed to have a cast-iron skull. She stopped in her tracks, swayed drunkenly, and the New Zealander, cat-footed, had her hitched to the big wagon before she knew what was happening. He went back quickly for the half-blind horse, placed her alongside her dazed companion, swung out of the farm gate, and walked and trotted both animals for a couple of miles down country lanes. The black mare reeled alarmingly from time to time, but she didn't fall, and she was in no condition to bolt. He got her back into the stable still half-dazed, and repeated the process next day. The vicious horse forgot her lesson, rushed at him once again in a raging fury as soon as he opened the stable door, and took another blow on the head which this time brought her down on one foreleg.

She didn't need the club on the third day. Natusch, very much on the alert, harnessed the mares to the farm mowing machine, and had mowed a couple of acres of hay before he noticed Frau Rueger watching him from a corner of the field. The Frau knew that her hay would be lost if it stood much longer, but her expression didn't change. She turned on her heel, and Natusch went on mowing. He was feeling relaxed and content, relieved that his battle with the black mare was over and done with, aware that his stay at Gaas was now no longer threatened. The mowing machine, Herr Rueger's prized possession, was working faultlessly, and he could smell the ripe grass as it tumbled before the sharp cutters. The war, which hadn't yet finished with him, receded into the background as a mild nostalgia supplanted it. It was for all the world as if he were back home in New Zealand.

The two horses seemed to share in his mood and his well-being. They pulled with a will, revelling in their freedom from the close confines of the stable, responding to his encouragement, making their harness jingle as they leaned powerfully into the traces, snatching an occasional mouthful of the lush grass, and keeping the reciprocating blade of the mower singing at high pitch.

They had another acre cut before Frau Rueger reappeared. She didn't smile, nor congratulate Natusch, nor ask questions, but she had with her a full flask of wine and a sizeable piece of homemade cake. The New Zealander acccepted the peace-offering gravely, said 'Danke, Frau Rueger,' as if it were nothing out of the ordinary, and resumed mowing. He noted the restrained bewilderment on his employer's face, and smiled briefly to himself. The risk he had taken had paid off. The hay was being won, the black horse was working hard, apparently none the worse for a bruised skull, the Frau was baffled but was doing her best not to show it, and he had had a bonus of wine and cake. He shook the reins and gave a cheerful 'Hup! Hup!' to the willing mares. All told, he felt, it hadn't been a bad day.

The black mare submitted to the daily harnessing after that without protest and without any evidence of evil intention, and she justified Herr Rueger's boast that she could work as well as any two ordinary horses; but she wasn't yet finished with this battle of wills. Her seeming docility fooled Natusch, who forgot that she also had the intelligence of two ordinary horses, and that she was inherently vicious. After a few days he discarded the club which he had carried whenever he was near her, and the mare, perhaps watching for it, celebrated his mistake by going for him open-mouthed and with ears flat once again.

This time, she very nearly had him. She would have trampled him into the ground in her rage, but for a desperate last-second punch on the muzzle which sobered her as abruptly as the club had done. The punch almost broke the New Zealander's hand, but it hurt the mare far worse. A horse's muzzle is sensitive, far more sensitive than a fist. A light blow can cause discomfort, even distress, and this was a full-blooded punch with every last ounce of the New Zealander's weight behind it. It was a murderous blow, and it was probably at this point that the black mare accepted defeat.

In a sense, her capitulation was inevitable. One of them, after all, had to go under in this battle of attrition, and during the last week the black horse had been savagely ill-used. She was now in excruciating pain. She stood still, tossing her head in mute agony, lifting her front feet high off the ground one at a time as spasms shook her, her smashed, bleeding forelip twitching convulsively, her raging spirit suddenly wholly subdued. Waves of shock flowed visibly over her body.

Natusch felt instinctively that this was the end, that she had taken enough punishment. He stood in front of her, whitefaced, the retrieved club in his sound hand, ready to fell her if she offered another challenge: but none came. The mare's spirit was broken; the fight had gone out of her. It was cruel, desperate treatment, and the New Zealander knew it, and all along had wanted no part of it, but he *had* to master this animal. If there had been an option, any option, he would have seized it.

The other mare, the gentle one, needed no rebukes. Her nature, which had survived far crueller treatment at the hands of the Obergefreiter, was still essentially affectionate. Natusch responded to it. He left her bridle on permanently, avoided her blind side, and talked to her softly and patiently whenever he had time. She gave him dumb thanks from the sound eye and began turning her head to welcome him whenever he approached her stall. He rubbed both horses down daily, fed special tit-bits to the black horse by way of atonement, and began talking to her, too, in the same half-endearing, half-abrasive tone which he used with her companion. It was a forlorn attempt to win her trust – and her pardon – and predictably, it failed. She ignored the encouragement, but she no longer kicked, nor gave evil glances, and she continued to work well. It seemed that her viciousness was spent, at least for the present. Natusch had to be content with that.

Frau Rueger remained completely mystified at the change in the daily routine: but she was too proud to ask questions, and Natusch offered no explanation. He brought in the rest of the hay crop, hauled the winter wood back to the farm, accepted the bonus which now came to him daily, and harnessed and worked the mares with an easy nonchalance that brought disbelieving frowns to his employer's face. She knew nothing of the club, nothing of the struggle which had taken place. She did know that until now, no one except the Obergefreiter himself had ever worked these two mares as a team, and she knew too that there wasn't a man in the village, or in the whole neighbourhood for that matter, who would dare go near the wild one. And yet here was this young British *Kriegsgefangener* treating it with even more disdain than her husband. She put it down to black magic. Some of the local farmers who came specially to see the devil horse working placidly under an alien hand shook their heads at the sight and endorsed her opinion.

Natusch didn't argue with them. His ruthless conquest of the black mare meant that he was now indispensable to Frau

Rueger, particularly during this present harvest period, and meant, too, that he'd be staying at Gaas, which again was imperative.

This wasn't a chance assignment for him, or for Sergeant Dai Davies, who was already working hard on his maps. Farm work was preferable to life in the Stalag by any standard, and Gaas was a pleasant village that took some of the sting out of their German captivity: but there was another more important, more prosaic attraction to the place which had brought them there specially and for one purpose only. Gaas lay a tantalizing half-hour's walk from the heavily patrolled Hungarian border.

CHAPTER TWO

OVER THE BORDER

The two horses raised their heads as Natusch walked through the stable door. He disregarded the mute appeal of the grey mare, retrieved the crowbar he had hidden in her stall, and emerged from his reverie as the half-blind animal made fresh demands that were too insistent to be ignored. He straightened up, smoothed her flanks with long sweeping strokes of his hand, noted the instant surrender which followed, and felt a real regret well up inside him. This was the last time he would be cosseting her, he reflected. Maybe he shouldn't have made so much of this horse, shouldn't have fussed over her the way he had done. She would pine for him, would go off her feed perhaps, certainly would have no one who would go on tempering the outrage that Herr Rueger had perpetrated.

He frowned, and glanced at the black mare in the adjoining stall. She had made no demands on him, had not deigned to acknowledge him. And what would happen to her, he wondered? He had been at the farm for just over four weeks now, and his mastery over the devil horse had remained unassailed. The question was – would anyone else be able to continue it? Or would Frau Rueger, in the end, in desperation, have to shoot her?

Natusch moved over, groomed the black mare carefully and thoroughly, replenished her hay and water, failed yet again to get any response, and gave her stablemate the same final, meticulous attention. Then, without a backward look, he picked up his crowbar and walked out of the stable. The mares would have to take their chance, he told himself, would have to make the best of it. He tried hard to control his growing ill-ease. The bigger issue that was now at hand allowed no room for sentiment: certainly not for the continued welfare of two mares.

Frau Rueger made no protest as Natusch set off for the billets an hour early. Of late, she had begun to worry lest he should ask for a transfer, and thus leave her with a pair of idle horses that no one else could do anything with; and he had done nothing to allay her fears. He smiled at her, the crowbar safely hidden under his clothes, acknowledged a respectful 'Guten Abend, Herr Natusch,' and left the farm.

The walk back to the billets was a pleasant one, despite the weather and a lingering sadness about the mares. Natusch turned up his collar against the increasing coldness of the November afternoon and strode along briskly, his feet crunching on the surface of the narrow lane. He breasted a slight hill, paused to take in the view, and away in the distance discerned a farm wagon emerging from a clump of trees somewhere near the border. He looked again, harder this time, wondering fleetingly if the two tiny figures he could see were Dai Davies and Herr Wolfgang Bauer.

The New Zealander walked on, a sudden grin appearing on his face. If it were Dai, he mused, he would no doubt be listening, as usual, to the voluble Wolfgang. The Welshman had been assigned as a labourer to Herr Bauer, the local forester, and there had been an instant bonus to this extraordinary stroke of luck. Ever since Dai had got the job, much of the forestry work had been done almost within hailing distance of the border – occasionally only a few yards from it – and so far he had hardly had need to ask a single question.

Herr Bauer, a jolly rotund man, and given to sweating profusely at the least effort, had showered his newly conscripted helper with information and confidences from their first meeting. He was a compulsive talker, as garrulous as Frau Rueger was withdrawn, and four weeks had so far failed to dam the flow; but, as Dai was quick to insist, he was never boring. It was, he affirmed, very much the reverse. On their first day together, the astonished Welsh sergeant had found himself listening to full details of the forester's private and very personal difficulties with his wife, and of his successful dalliance with a lady whose husband was away at the war. The frequent bulletins which followed these initial disclosures never failed to bring the broadest of grins to Herr Bauer's face, nor to Dai's either, but female conquest was only one of the German's many interests; and for all his garullity, he compelled attention. He conversed lengthily and with a surprising amount of expertise about the war, he outlined the strategy that the High Command would employ in Russia if they had any grain of sense at all, he lectured Dai on conifers and how to grow them successfully – Herr Bauer really did know his subject here – and went on cheerfully and knowledgeably about wine, agreed that it was the cause of much of his copious sweating, but urged Dai, with sudden ear-to-ear grins, not to forget his paramour's contribution. He also talked a lot about his forestry service and a little about the nearby frontier.

Dai listened patiently and for the most part with real interest to a torrent of dubious anecdote and genuine information. He could speak German tolerably well, and had no real difficulty, even with colloquialisms, but he seemed frequently a shade slow to grasp his employer's references to the frontier. Herr Bauer, responsive to almost any cue, elaborated willingly, and all too often produced more fact and local knowledge than Dai could cope with.

The Welshman memorized as much as he could. He took all the detail he could carry back with him to the billets, got out his hidden maps and set to work. So far, he had redrawn the maps twice to accommodate more and yet more roads, paths, sentry-boxes, copses and even ditches in exact and minute detail; but they didn't extend beyond the border. Dai had put out a feeler very tentatively here, found that Herr Bauer wasn't over-interested, and had deemed it wise not to press the point.

Natusch watched the wagon disappear behind a clump of trees before resuming his journey to the billets. He walked quickly, his heart warming to the voluble and lecherous German forester. Crossing the border would be no easy matter after all, as Dai had found out, but all unsuspectingly, Herr Bauer had now covered this vital part of their escape plan. His help was timely. They had a thousand-mile trek ahead of them, and as Dai had remarked more than once, they would look damn stupid if they were to mess up the first leg of it.

The New Zealander's thoughts turned to another, equally important matter. The food problem, he reflected, which at first had threatened an unconscionable delay, had been solved almost as easily and fortuitously as the border mapping. Luck, it seemed, was with them for the present, as this even more significant good fortune had proved. Serious escapers shun contact with all and sundry, and take their supplies from whatever base they are leaving: but initially the Gaas commando had offered Davies and Natusch no help at all. It held none of the ubiquitous Red Cross parcels, and it hadn't seen any for six weeks. There wasn't a crumb in the place: but again, their star was ascending. A flood of deliveries had arrived towards the end of October, and a store of concentrates and food tins was now hidden in the billets. It was safe there. There hadn't been a snap search in the whole three years' history of the Gaas commando.

There wasn't, of course, any reason why the place should be searched. Gaas billets wasn't a prison lager in the accepted sense of the term. It was an old-fashioned, thick-walled house set on the outskirts of the village, and none of its twenty-five occupants had yet toyed with the idea of burrowing a tunnel to the outside. There was no need for one. The British prisoners worked on farms in the locality, mostly without supervision, and any one of them could walk away at any time he chose. None of them had done so. Most of the men were well treated, in some cases had been accepted as one of the family, and the anomaly of a dual loyalty had inevitably arisen. The same thing was happening in England, in Italy, in many countries. Newly formed parochial and personal ties were being added to an existing patriotism which in most cases was not diminished and was in no way debased. It is unlikely that the men concerned explored the phenomenon in any depth, but they were not the least interested in escaping, and in fairness, no discredit could be attached to them. The few at Gaas who had thought about leaving still didn't go. They knew that the difficulty wasn't in getting away but in staying away.

The house itself was secure. An edict, issued by the Kriegsgefangenen-Abteilung, the Wehrmacht's P.O.W. section, had instructed that prisoners in rural areas were to be rigorously confined at night-time, and steel bars now guarded the window of the house, and the back and side doors had been bricked up. Each evening an elder Deutscher Volkssturmer closed the single remaining front door, which opened outwards, and padlocked a heavy iron bar across it to staples embedded in the wall on either side. He didn't avail himself, the two new men noticed, of the extra protection of the old-fashioned lock guarding the door itself, which somehow seemed a good omen. The lock was a simple affair and wouldn't have delayed them overlong, but the iron bar outside was a very different proposition. Once its padlocks were snapped home, no one could get out of the building – nor into it – until morning, when the Home Guard man reappeared. The counter to this formidable barrier, once they had thought of it, and for experienced men they were a long time in the thinking, seemed almost too elementary to be true.

Natusch stopped at the door of the billets, checked that no one was watching, and brought out the hidden crowbar. It took only a few seconds to wrench out the key staple, the one farthest from the door hinges, and a minute or two more to replace it, and to wedge it so that the manoeuvre would pass unnoticed. That was all he had to do. He checked his handiwork, noticed with approval the ever-increasing coldness of the afternoon, and went into the billets.

Dai Davies came back with the rest of the working contingent an hour later. He lifted a questioning eyebrow, accepted Natusch's answering nod, and without more ado settled down to enjoy his evening meal. Dai had excellent nerves. Neither man mentioned the coming escape, nor the repercussions which were bound to follow. That subject had already been well covered. 'It won't make any difference to them,' Dai had insisted. 'These chaps have been here for about two years now, and none of them has ever put a foot wrong. Not so far as I know, anyway. They won't get blamed. They won't get moved, either. The farmers'll soon quash that idea. We're newcomers, so when the Jerries have done shouting, they'll just have to accept that they made a bad choice.' Dai grinned. 'One thing *will* happen, though. That's for sure. They'll fix that damn door good and proper.'

The evening passed more sedately than the two men had anticipated. A huge fire, burning in the big iron stove in the centre of the room, and constantly replenished with rough-hewn blocks of wood, radiated its warmth comfortably to the farthest corners. Natusch glanced around. His fellow prisoners were sitting on their beds or at the big table, mostly in their shirt sleeves, relaxing after the day's work, chatting about local affairs and farming matters, and occasionally about home and the unusual severity of the weather. Their pleasant idyll was yet to be shattered.

Outside, it was perishingly cold. During the past week, an iron frost had descended, had gripped the ground day and night, had killed all hope of further ploughing, and had kept sentries everywhere huddled in their boxes. Each night the moon emerged, pale and wan, to accentuate the cold and to make escaping conditions perfect. It was the kind of weather that gave hot meals and a warm bed precedence over all other considerations, and neither Davies nor Natusch were surprised at the reception which greeted their invitation.

They had long since agreed that an invitation would have to be made. There would only ever be one escape from Gaas, which meant that they had to give anyone – if there was anyone – with ideas similar to their own a sporting chance. Halfway through the evening Dai stood up. 'We're leaving,' he announced briefly. 'Tonight. Natusch and me. If any of you chaps want to come with us, you're welcome.'

The sergeant's clear voice stilled the hubbub of the room instantly. Card games ceased, cups halted in mid-air, and conversations froze. Dai, calm and assured, watched the varying reactions of his fellow-prisoners. Some of them thought he was joking, and smiled vaguely, unable to see the point of his jest; a few, who had observed the stockpiling of food tins, felt an instant concern for his safety, and the silence broke as they began doing their best to dissuade him; others, not yet grasping fully what had been said, but sensing the atmosphere, wore looks that ranged from incomprehension to near-panic. 'But you *can't* go now,' one man protested incredulously. Astonishment made his voice squeak. 'Not in this weather. You'll have to sleep out. Christ, you'll freeze to death!'

There was only one dissenter, which confirmed a feeling that Natusch had had all along. He was Joe Walker, a private of the 51st Highland Division, a chunky little man with wide shoulders, who made the decision to give everyone an even chance seem worthwhile. 'I'll come,' he said. He spoke quietly and dourly. 'I had an idea you might be going. My pack's ready. And thanks for telling me.'

Surprisingly, no one said any more after that. Worried frowns and astonished looks gradually wore away, card games restarted, and presently the room regained some of its casual camaraderie; but the unease remained. Towards eight o'clock the guard came in. It was freezing harder than ever, he said. He failed to notice the sudden tenseness of the room, counted his Kriegsgefangenen slowly and painstakingly, and eventually – unwillingly, it seemed – left the warm billets and went stamping out.

They didn't leave until ten o'clock. They had to wait that long for Gaas to settle down and for errant villagers to find their way home; but waiting was a dreary business. Conversation became unreal and stilted, until it ebbed, leaving a feeling of emptiness, almost of embarrassment: but the waiting continued. It was part of the plan, and despite the discomfort and edginess of being poised too long, the village clock tolled its full quota before anyone moved.

They got up as the last chime sounded, and approached the door. Joe Walker hung back a little, apprehensive, aware that somehow a solid oak door, bolted and barred, was to be breached, intrigued as to what kind of a miracle would now be wrought.

His nerves were promptly given their first test. Natusch pushed a length of wire through the window, lassooed the iron bar, held it so that it wouldn't fall, and nodded to Davies. The Welshman gave the door a tentative push with his shoulder. Nothing happened. He tried again, harder this time, but the door remained firm. Natusch had jammed the staple with a piece of wood and the night air had swollen the wedge. Joe Walker looked on, frowning, wholly bewildered at this seemingly puny effort to overcome such a barrier. Dai grinned to himself as he allowed the tension to rise still higher. If he kept this up long enough, he thought, perhaps the new man would have the grace to look worried.

But there was no time for levity. Dai glanced a warning at Natusch and then put his weight behind another assault. Joe's eyes widened in disbelief as the door opened, suddenly, smoothly, and as a foot or so of the restraining wire disappeared through the window. Dai edged outside, stopped the bar from clattering to the ground, and grinned again. 'It's simple, really,' he confessed to Joe Walker. The new man's incredulity had now turned satisfactorily to blank astonishment. 'It's mind over matter, y'know. We hypnotized the guard, of course.'

Dai and Joe waited dutifully for Natusch at the gate of the billets. Thoughtful escapers don't make the gaolers a gift of their exit method, and before he left, the New Zealander had the door once again barred and the staple firmly entrenched in its socket. No amount of pushing would move it now. If the men who were snoring away inside the building could manage to keep dumb about it, he speculated, it would be some little time before the authorities solved this mystery.

The lager could have been better sited. Its gate opened on to the main street of the village, and they kept a strict *qui vive* as they crossed the empty highway and walked quickly through a gap between the two houses opposite down to the river bank. Their route to the frontier was planned meticulously. Davies and Natusch had checked it a dozen times, and all except the incalculable had been considered and due allowance made: but blind chance very nearly spoilt everything before they had covered the first half-mile.

They walked along the river bank to a bridge, and stopped in the shadow of some trees to listen. In the mill house on the other side of the river was a permanent guard who was supposed to be doing a night shift watching the bridge; but they knew this German well. He was a cheerful character, a veteran of the '14–'18 conflict, and he hadn't been impressed when the local Fuehrers had told him that his rickety bridge was an outpost of the Grossdeutsche Reich. It was an odds-against chance, they felt, that their realist friend would be anywhere other than in his mill, sitting by a warm fire: but he was still a risk. They listened, and heard nothing except the ripple of water and the occasional sighing of wind through the trees. All was well. Dai Davies was on the point of emerging from the shadows when Natusch jerked savagely at his sleeve. 'Down!' he hissed. 'Someone coming!'

The Welshman dropped flat just in time. Along their side of the river, black against the sky, came a two-man Wehrmacht patrol, rifles slung from their shoulders, jackboots making surprisingly little noise against the frozen earth. They approached the narrow bridge, dropped into single file, passed less than a yard from the hidden Britishers, missed seeing them by some miracle that no one attempted to understand, clumped noisily over the bridge and vanished.

The trio gave them five minutes grace before tiptoeing after them and plunging into the comforting anonymity of ploughed fields. The encounter had shaken them. It had shaken Natusch, particularly. The border was now only a mile away, and he found himself tingling with all the old fears and exhilaration of a dozen previous escapes.

But the night was young, and held surprises in plenty. The next was an abrupt and inexplicable weather change that sent rain misting down to loosen the hard grip of the frost and to make the top crust of earth even more treacherous and slippery than before. At first it was no hardship. The three men drew nearer the border, picked up their bearings accurately, and began following a ditch that they knew would lead eventually to a point mid-way between two sentry-boxes. Here, on the precise borderline between the two countries, it was imperative to maintain a really vigilant alert. Hungary was now the wealthiest country in Europe, and nationals of both sides were engaged in the lucrative business of smuggling. The frontier guards knew all about the illicit trade. They had dogs – killer dogs, it was rumoured – they got a bonus for each smuggler caught, and some of them, if rumour was to be believed, had few scruples as to how the capture was effected.

In normal weather, crossing the border would have been dangerous enough, but this night was to hold overmuch unpleasantness. The ditch they were following was one of a network of ditches, and it had needed careful planning to find the best route. Second right and third left would have brought them to the right spot, but it was now almost pitch dark, and rain was blurring the outline of the hedges. They walked in single file, Dai Davies leading, their senses keyed for danger. Suddenly Dai stopped. Ten yards ahead of him was something solid, a deeper shadow against the background of darkness. He thought it was a tree, but no tree of this size had figured in his calculations.

The Welshman moved forward to investigate, picking his way carefully and silently over the muddy ground. He came back as carefully, but faster, and made violent back-pedalling gestures that needed no explanation. The 'tree' was one of the sentry-boxes that at all costs they had to avoid. They backed off like three wraiths, counted ninety paces parallel with the frontier and moved forward again towards the narrow track that was the patrol beat.

By now, a stroke of luck was overdue; and possibly because they hadn't complained as much as they might have done, a measure of good fortune was granted. No guards saw them cross the patrol beat into Hungary, and they got there without a pack of dogs yelping at their heels; but they didn't cross noiselessly. Rain was beating down hard now, and the ploughed no-man's-land on each side of the border had become something of a morass. Each time Natusch lifted a foot from the ground, it left a hole he could have buried a cat in. The three miles across country to the first woods of Hungary were hard going too, but they still didn't complain. With all this wet and mud around, not even a bloodhound would be able to follow their tracks.

The first stage of the escape was now over. The three men stopped in the woods, rested a while, and then pushed on at full speed, crossing fields, skirting villages, getting as far away from the border as they could before dawn. Towards three o'clock in the morning, the frost regained its grip, and soon the ground was crunching again beneath their tread. They went due east, heading for the interior, checking their direction occasionally against the illuminated dial of the little stud compass that by now had survived half a dozen searches.

They spent the day concealed in a patch of thick undergrowth in the middle of a wood. It wasn't a comfortable day, nor a warm one, and water dripped continually from overhanging branches, but they endured it all cheerfully. The German had a long arm, and they weren't yet beyond his reach.

But even the dullest of days has some moment to enliven it. Occasional carts creaked by on unseen paths through the wood, and sometimes peasants' voices reached them. Halfway through the morning a rustling of leaves made them look up sharply, but the intrusion brought no menace. Five fawn deer came racing through the trees, stopped and browsed in a glade near them, until, catching the alien scent, they flung off at a mad gallop. Somehow, that incident, perhaps because of the breath of real liberty that it carried, kept them in good heart all day.

They set off again at dusk. At first, a bright moon lit the way over frosted fields and through still more woods, but the weather was doing its best to unsettle them. Towards midnight the sky grew overcast and rain began falling again.

They kept going, using the compass frequently, intent on putting in at least twenty miles before dawn.

They didn't make it. A river, fifty yards wide, deep and fast-flowing, was one reason; increasing cold and showers of sleet another. They followed the bank of the river, trying to find a bridge, and were turned back at the outskirts of a village by a frenzy of barking dogs. They retreated, went back past their starting point, and after another half-mile found the bridge: but its discovery did them no good. It was a railway bridge, and this time the sentry was alert. He called on them to halt, fired a warning shot, and then a burst as they went racing away over sodden fields.

There was no pursuit. They stopped, panting, water running in streams from their greatcoats, wondering what to do now. If they'd been dedicated escapers, they'd have gone on, but when Natusch looked questioningly at Walker and Davies, no response came to buoy his own flagging spirits. They were all too cold and too weary to care for anything except rest, and perhaps a little warmth.

Dai Davies came to the point admirably. 'We'll flake out if we go on much longer,' he said. 'Let's find a barn and get out of this damned rain.'

Joe Walker, the dour one, agreed promptly. Conditions must have been bad. 'Best thing,' he remarked. 'I'm out on my feet.'

They found their barn. It was built on to the end of a large farmhouse, and none of the dogs heard them as they crept into it. They stayed hidden the whole of the next day, their second day in Hungary, slept a lot, caught up with delayed meals, and used part of the long waiting hours to settle a matter of policy. For some time now, Davies and Natusch had been considering the advantage of adopting a commissioned rank in the event of their being arrested by the Hungarian military. A commission would ease a good many of the difficulties which would ensue if that happened, but they recognized that it might also bring problems in its wake. The fact that neither of them was wearing officer's uniform was their least worry. A British officer who was determined to escape from the first moment of capture might well choose to identify himself to the Wehrmacht as an ordinary soldier – suitably attired, of course – and thus avoid the stringent security of an Oflag. That was plausible enough. It was a ruse which had been employed many times already in many different armies, and it meant that the reverse explanation should be accepted without demur. It was possible that the question might not even arise. They looked beyond it, examined the real difficulties which would follow if, by mischance, the Hungarians were to send them back, as officers, to their allies in the Reich, and agreed that probable German reaction was an acceptable risk. They also concurred that one commissioned rank would suit the proposed deception better than two, but were still at odds, despite all their discussions, as to which of them should assume it. The question of ethics, if there was such a question, didn't bother them at all. If any armchair warrior wanted to argue about military usage and protocol once they got back, he was welcome, they felt, and good luck to him.

Natusch broached the matter once again. 'About this officer business, Dai,' he began tentatively. He was anxious to get the affair settled. 'Look, you're a sergeant, Joe and I are only privates. You're the senior chap here, so it's up to you. How about we agree on that now, and stop arguing?'

But Dai wouldn't have it. 'No,' he disclaimed. 'Not me.' He spoke emphatically. 'We've been over all this before. You know that. I am a sergeant, true enough, but you keep forgetting that I'm a regular, too. Been one all my life. That lets me out.' An upturned hand silenced Natusch. 'Like I've said,' Dai went on, 'to be an officer, to look like one, that is, you've got to be either a duration-only wallah with six weeks O.C.T.U. behind you, or a real professional. They're the only types that take their commission for granted. There's some of both sorts who look bloody fools as well, but even then, you can tell the pips are genuine. No, I couldn't do it. I've been a soldier too long.' He looked quizzically at Natusch. 'I don't suppose you've had any officer training,' he went on, 'but you've already pushed yourself up to corporal, and no one's been any the wiser. There's nothing that I know of to stop you going higher.' He ignored an embryo protest. 'Major,' he mused. He shook his head. 'No, too high. They'd smell a rat. You'd better be a captain, Roy.' Dai levelled a warning finger. 'And that's the end of it,' he said firmly. 'I'm getting fed up with this topic.' He grinned and brought up an arm in mock salute. 'Sir, Sergeant Davies reporting. A decision has now been reached, sir. At last, sir. And about bloody time too, sir.'

Natusch didn't argue further. Dai Davies was adamant that he wouldn't have the job, Joe Walker was first to admit that it didn't suit him, and one of them, they were agreed, would have to assume commissioned rank if the Hungarians were to catch up with them. Being honest about it, the New Zealander found himself welcoming the possible promotion. Decisions might yet depend on him because of it, and where escaping was concerned, he liked to trust his own judgment.

During the long day a feeble light illumined the loft, but as evening wore on it reverted slowly to almost total darkness. It was no hardship. They waited, comfortable and content, and let the hours slip by without feeling any urge to prod them. There was enough walking ahead without rushing at it.

The three men left the barn soon after dusk, and that night everything went their way. They kept clear of roads, but ploughed fields soon gave way to pastureland, and they marched steadily hour after hour for the best part of thirty miles. No one saw them, and the following night brought the same fortune and carried them the same distance. Natusch felt elated. Another day or two at this pace would put them well beyond the reach of any German tentacles.

They set off earlier on the fifth day, travelling south now, heading on a wide dog-leg course towards Yugoslavia, and dawn found them at the edge of an oak and beech forest, with the hilly country behind them. It was once again freezing. Ahead lay the broad plain through which the Danube flowed; far to the east, and still over a hundred miles distant, were the twin cities of Buda and Pest.

Dai Davies voiced a suggestion that was overdue, and which was accepted before the last word left his mouth. 'I think we've come far enough,' he ventured. 'How about lighting a fire and having a hot breakfast?' He added unnecessary encouragement. 'And getting warm?'

They drew back into the forest and stopped at a pile of neatly-cut stakes. Those beneath the top layer were dry, and presently they had a fire crackling, bacon sizzling in a dixie-lid, and a can of water rapidly approaching the boil with a double handful of tea gyrating over its surface in characteristic whorls.

It was a perfect meal. The three escapers ate their fill in an almost reverent silence and then lay back puffing contentedly at cigarettes and revelling in the warmth of the fire. Natusch, enjoying the glow that was travelling pleasantly up his legs, beamed at his friends. He felt no inkling of danger, no uneasiness, no premonition that capture was imminent.

CHAPTER THREE

ENTER STRANGERS

Capture is perhaps too strong a word. The three fugitives had realized from the beginning that their idea of gaining the Yugoslav border unhindered and of then joining the Partisans was an optimistic one. The odds were against it. They would probably run into the Hungarian police or military eventually, and their main concern so far had been to put as many miles as they could between themselves and the German-influenced border squads before the Hungarians caught up with them. After that, willy-nilly, they would have to test the rumour that in Hungary, escaped prisoners received treatment which by normal standards was both welcome and unorthodox.

The warm fire, with its soporific effect, was the real culprit. Dai Davies was suggesting to the chunky Joe Walker that it wouldn't harm any of them if he were to brew another can of tea, when, without warning, the forest exploded Hungarians. There were about thirty of them, women as well as men, and they came from all angles. The fugitives stood up, aware that one or two of the men were carrying shotguns, conscious that unpleasant things could happen.

For a long moment no one moved. One of the armed Hungarians then stepped forward, asked in German who they were, and clicked his tongue in surprise at the answer 'Englander Kriegsgefangenen.' He followed up with more questions, examined their clothes and escape packs carefully, looked hard at each of the three men in turn, and then, making up his mind abruptly, offered his hand. A sudden tension relaxed. The peasants, all thirty of them, took their cue from the spokesman, mobbed the relieved trio, shook their hands vigorously, and after a few minutes of voluble and incomprehensible chatter, led them in what appeared to be a heroes' march to their village.

From there events moved fast. A couple of gendarmes with roosters' tails in their hats arrived before midday, and announced through an interpreter that they were the official escort. They didn't say where to or on whose orders, and an hour later, the three ex-Gaas men found themselves in a railway carriage, still uncertain of what was going to happen, and with the stud compass at the ready to tell them.

The gendarmes were no help at all. They sat on the seat opposite, loosened their revolver belts, and beamed a cheerful ignorance of German, English, Italian and French. No one but they knew Hungarian, so the uncertainty remained. Natusch nudged Dai Davies as the train started. 'Not so good, son,' he said briefly. 'We're heading west. Towards Germany.'

But Dai didn't panic. 'Maybe,' he agreed. There was a half-grin on his face. 'But Germany's a hundred miles away, and we're not there yet.' He regarded Natusch unemotionally. 'We may have to crown these fellows and hop out, but let's not be too hasty. Leave it until we're ten miles from the border. It could be they're doing us a good turn.'

Dai's hunch was right. Three hours later, the train stopped at the garrison town of Szombathely, and the two escorts intimated that they weren't going any farther. Natusch felt a sharp sense of relief. The reprieve had come just in time. The garrison was situated twenty-five miles east of Austria and only fifteen miles remained before the assault and exit plan would have gone into action.

Szombathely H.Q. was an efficient place. The gendarmes left them at the guardhouse, and a few minutes later, a lieutenant who spoke English, and who knew that he was to receive a British officer and two other ranks, walked into the room. Natusch greeted him perfunctorily. He was unsure as to the kind of reception that would be offered, and a touch of Prussian stiffness, he felt, might well bolster his status and affirm the new rank. He examined the register which the officer had brought, and signed it as Captain Roy Spencer Natusch, No. 3995, of the New Zealand Expeditionary Force.

The unofficial promotion paid a spot dividend. He was given special facilities for washing, insisted successfully that

Dai and Joe were to stay with him, and was shown a deference that wasn't extended towards them. The lieutenant was very friendly. He ordered drinks – two glasses – and congratulated Natusch on escaping. 'You are the first British officer we've had in Hungary,' he commented. He was wrong there, although neither of them knew it. The New Zealander was the second British 'officer' to arrive in Hungary, and the first, a genuine colonel, was at that moment in Budapest, engaged on a very delicate task indeed.

Natusch gave the lieutenant his attention. 'Your status here is rather unusual,' he was saying. 'We haven't replied yet to your country's declaration of war, so officially you're not an enemy of Hungary. But you're hardly a friend, and we owe a duty to our German ally.' He drained his glass and signalled the mess orderly. 'I think we'll ignore that duty,' he went on lightly. 'Tomorrow, you and your men are going to Komorom. It's an old fortress we are using as a reception centre for aliens, and I'm told it's quite a good place. You'll be staying there for a while as involuntary guests of our country. Komorom,' the officer concluded, 'is sixty kilometres from Budapest.'

Natusch's doubts about Komorom were well founded. During the last two years, he had seen the inside of a dozen camps and over a score of jails and prison cells, and he'd grown wary of those that were praised in advance. They were usually the rough places, and Komorom, as he'd feared, was no exception. With one difference. He was now an officer, and he was prepared to use the rank to advantage.

He got no opportunity to do so on the first evening. It was a long train journey, in the right direction, and this time free from any anxiety as to where it might finish. They arrived at the fortress just after dusk, and the interrogation squad who kept the three of them for a couple of hours made no move to produce the Kommandant. There was no difficulty with the interrogators. Natusch, now the accepted spokesman, told them exactly how they had won free, and kept quiet only about his sudden promotion. He should, he reflected too late, have asked a few questions about the fortress, and demanded an inspection of his quarters, but he forgot. The office they were sitting in was warm and comfortable, and he assumed, as did Dai and Joe, that their own accommodation would at least be tolerable.

They made a bad mistake. A guard escorted them from the interrogation office and led them through low, ill-lit rooms that seemed full of men in almost the last stages of degradation. Natusch gathered from the interpreter that they were Russian and Polish ex-prisoners-of-war, and they made a depressing sight. Some of them were asleep on the dirty straw which littered the floor, whilst others sat apathetically, taking no notice of the newcomers. They were mostly dressed in shabby trousers and jackets and many were barefoot. Dai Davies found an English-speaking Pole, and learnt that these conditions were general throughout the fortress.

It didn't augur well for their own accommodation, but the room they were shown into seemed at first to be reasonable. The three men who were already there got up to greet them. Two were English soldiers who had escaped from Germany, and whom the new men were to know briefly. The third, the spokesman of the trio, was a Hungarian Jew from Palestine who had Anglicized his name to Tom Sanders, and who was to claim a part – a tragic one – in the events that were drawing nearer.

Sanders had already got himself a third nationality. He was now a British subject, and a volunteer soldier as well, with a touching faith in British Army officers in general, and in their ability to remedy injustice in particular.

He lost no time in making his appeal to the New Zealander. 'Glad to see you, sir,' he began. He fingered his ragged clothing with distaste. 'I'm afraid we don't look respectable, sir, but this is the best we can do. We've nothing else to wear. The Kommandant keeps promising us new clothes, but I don't believe we'll get any. He says we're all going to a new camp – a good one – very soon, but I don't believe that, either. We've been here a fortnight now, and there's no sign of a move. Sir, the food's bad, there's no blankets and no bug-powder, but there are bugs. This place is full of them.' Sanders stopped, took a needed breath, and finished his report. 'I don't think you'll like it here, sir, but I'm glad you've come.'

Natusch couldn't say that he echoed Tom Sanders' joy. In war, brutality and degradation are inevitable, but no man is anxious to get mixed up with them more than he has to. He banished the thought, turned to Sanders, and noticed the marks of bug bites on his body and the spaniel look in his eyes. To this man, he realized, he was no less than God-sent. A fully-fledged British officer wouldn't tolerate living in a hole like this for long, and when he left, he'd take his men with him. It was as simple as that. The relief and anticipation in Sanders' eyes made it clear that he already considered the problem as solved. For his own part, Natusch began to realize that there was more to a commission than he or Dai Davies or Joe Walker had suspected.

The New Zealander took Sanders with him next morning to the Kommandant's office. Relays of bugs had very nearly eaten him alive during the night and he was in a foul temper. He glanced at Sanders trying to assess the man's character. What he intended to say to this damned jail boss, when he met him, would need a good interpreter who wouldn't be afraid to translate literally.

The Kommandant was middle-aged, on the fat side, and to Natusch's biased eye, distinctly shifty looking. He was also, surprisingly, only a lieutenant. Komorom, it seemed, didn't rate highly with the Hungarian military authorities.

He and Natusch exchanged salutes, shook hands perfunctorily, and got down to business. The New Zealander turned on the heat right away. 'Tell the Kommandant,' he instructed Sanders, 'that I am a British officer, and according to his superiors, to be regarded as a guest of Hungary. Point out, too, that I am above him in rank.' The lieutenant nodded agreement as Sanders cleared the decks. 'Don't wrap this part up,' Natusch continued. 'Tell him that I am disgusted at the way in which I have been received here, and that I intend to take up this matter strongly: that it is not only his lack of respect for me to which I take exception, but also the insult to my country. Tell him, too, that I have noted how he is treating British, Polish and Russian soldiers, and that I am making a full report as soon as possible, and that I am naming him as the officer responsible. Has he anything to say to that?'

The Lieutenant had. Increasing alarm had crossed his face as the tirade progressed and as Natusch's gaze grew even more uncompromising and hostile, and Sanders had barely finished before the floodgates opened. Hungarians, as Sanders had explained to Natusch beforehand, are very officer- and honour-conscious, and the flamboyant speech had hit the right note. Added to that, the threat of a written report was already reminding the Kommandant forcibly that he had a job to lose.

He began talking. War, he explained, with a wealth of gesture, was a bestial thing, and mistakes were being made everywhere. His new guest's stay in a bug-ridden room, apparently, was one of the major ones. He was going on to say that henceforth the captain's well-being was something that he'd look after himself instead of leaving it to underlings, when Natusch interrupted. He hadn't expected such an easy victory as this, and it made him instantly suspicious, but having won it, it wasn't going to be wasted. If there were to be any specifications, he, Natusch, would make them. 'Tell the Kommandant,' he ordered Sanders, 'that tonight I shall sleep in a bed with sheets and blankets, as is customary to serving officers. He is to ensure personally that my room is clean and free from vermin. In addition, all prisoners—' he corrected himself '—all *ex*-prisoners in this fortress are to be given facilities for cleansing themselves and their quarters, and they are to receive adequate rations. Today.' Natusch was riding roughshod over the unhappy lieutenant. 'I don't wish to make too bad a report to the International Red Cross, or to the Kommandant's superiors,' he added, ending on a kinder note, 'so I will wait until I have made my inspection tomorrow morning before writing it.' He changed his more tolerant look for a scowl. 'I hope to be favourably impressed.'

The Kommandant's attitude confirmed that he had a lot to hide. He stood in front of Natusch, listened attentively as Sanders set out the outrageous demands, and his only reaction was an almost nauseating servility. The fat lieutenant was in a dilemma. So far, he'd only had to deal with prisoners who were either too complacent or too frightened to challenge him, but this new man, obviously, was an awkward and potentially dangerous customer who would need special handling. He could hardly be 'removed' – although the temptation was strong – because H.Q. had just sent him to Komorom, and they'd hardly forget about the transfer. Not yet awhile, anyway. Appeasement seemed the only answer.

The Kommandant laid it on thick and heavy. A private room, he said, would be prepared immediately, and a hot bath would be ready almost as soon as the captain was. He promised showers and a supply of soap for the men, and also proper food and fresh straw forthwith. There was, as Natusch knew, an acute shortage of blankets, so he passed the straw issue. Reverting once more to his guest, the now eager Hungarian promised English books, agreed that Dai Davies and Joe Walker should be billeted with Natusch, and capped his other bribes by offering a personal loan of 200 *pengös* to tide over any financial difficulty. That was a revealing gesture. Two hundred *pengös* were worth £10, and £10 is no light consideration to a mere lieutenant in any army, except, perhaps, to one engaged in the lucrative business of selling prisoners' rations. Natusch's suspicions of the fat officer vanished. They were confirmed, and a strong distaste came with them.

All the promises materialized. The private room was prepared, as were the incidentals, and that afternoon bonfires of dirty, vermin-infested straw burnt all over the fortress grounds. Natusch made his threatened inspection next morning, and was astonished at the abrupt change of morale in the Russian and Polish soldiers: but although he managed to improve conditions at Komorom beyond anyone's expectation, he found that he could do nothing to speed up transfers to 'good' camps. Not even for himself.

The reason was mainly political. There were three Polish officers in another part of the fortress who hadn't thought of brow-beating the Kommandant, and they helped Natusch to bring his political knowledge up to date. He heard once again, after they had finished congratulating him, that Hungary was more or less neutral, despite her alliance with Germany. There were no Wehrmacht troops in the country, and there were very few people outside the Arrow Cross movement who wanted it any different. The Arrow Cross was a pro-Nazi organization, but it had few members and was of small account. The government itself, Natusch gathered, was right-wing, and its sympathies were anti-German, to an extent that refugees who managed to get into Hungary not only received political asylum but also a large measure of freedom. The news hadn't yet penetrated the German Stalags to any degree, but it had travelled far in other directions, and there were now so many refugees in Hungary that accommodation was being strained to the limit. This, in a nutshell, explained Komorom and similar detention camps, and it wasn't hard to appreciate why transfers were difficult to arrange: nor why the fat lieutenant was nervous. He was on to a very lucrative racket indeed, and he didn't want it spoiled.

Natusch met the Kommandant several times during the next few days. On each occasion he was greeted like an old friend, and told, via Tom Sanders, that the camp he was bound for excelled all others in comfort and cuisine. That cut no ice at all. What did matter was the Hungarian's assurance that H.Q. didn't intend to separate Natusch from Dai Davies and Joe Walker. The New Zealander was relieved to hear that. The phoney rank, suggested by Dai, seconded by Joe, and worn by him, was communal property, and was their passport and their talisman to the safety of their own lines.

On the seventh day, the commandant sought out Natusch and invited him to his office. When he had finished hedging, the New Zealander gathered from the faintly perspiring prison chief that a Colonel Lorand Utassy of the XXI Department of the Hungarian War Office was coming to Komorom from Budapest that afternoon to see the newly arrived British officer, and he realized immediately the effect that this news must have had. The poor lieutenant was convinced that he had been 'shopped', and that a report had gone in after all. His relief, once he realized that Natusch had never heard of Utassy or the XXI Department, was so comical that the New Zealander almost forgave him that first dreadful night at the fortress.

He didn't realize, for a long time, the importance of Colonel Utassy's visit. A big Mercedes car drew up in the fortress grounds during the afternoon, and two men got out. One of them, immaculate in gold-braided uniform, was the Colonel. The other, in civilian clothes, was connected with the Foreign Office, but the significance of that escaped Natusch. The Colonel was all smiles. 'Ah! Captain Natusch!' he said breezily. His English had a barely noticeable accent. 'Glad to see you.' He shook hands, introduced his companion, and nodded briefly to the Kommandant.

The visit left Natusch baffled. He and his visitors spent over an hour in the Kommandant's office, drinking the brandy that was clearly a renewed peace offering, smoking

Colonel Utassy's American cigarettes, and chatting easily and very amicably about nothing in particular. After a while Natusch complimented Utassy on his excellent English. The Hungarian demurred. 'But I should speak it well,' he protested jovially. 'I was a military attaché in England for several years just before the war.' He drained his glass, and had it promptly refilled by the Kommandant. 'Tell me,' he went on, 'how did the Germans treat you as a prisoner? I've heard that they're a brutal lot.'

It went on like that. Natusch detailed his experiences in Germany, didn't mention rank or commissions, and answered one or two rather shrewd questions from the Foreign Office chap. He didn't ask Utassy why he had come or what he really wanted to know. He was content to sip liqueur brandy, smoke American cigarettes, and let his visitors make the running. They grew mellow as the bottle emptied, until at length even the Kommandant was at ease, but the conversation never rose above trivialities. It was obvious to the New Zealander that Utassy and his anonymous friend were vetting him, finding out what kind of a man he was, but why they were taking this trouble wasn't explained. It was clear that the new rank was not in dispute.

Only one item of importance emerged from the meeting. 'You won't be staying here for long,' Utassy said confidently. 'This place is only a reception camp, and it's not usual for officers to be here. I should imagine that your move will come through in a day or two. Your own men will travel with you, of course.' Apart from that, Natusch knew no more when the Colonel and his friend got back into their Mercedes than when they'd stepped out of it. But it was a big car, and it seemed reasonable to assume that they hadn't driven it all the way from Budapest to use up petrol.

The Kommandant brought the news two days later. 'It's just come through,' he said, again through the ubiquitous Sanders. 'Tomorrow you're going to Budapest, and from there to Szigetvar. That's a small town near the Yugoslav border.' A broad we're-all-pals-together smile nearly succeeded in masking the Kommandant's relief. 'I'm sorry you're going,' he went on. 'Yes, I'll miss you.'

Natusch looked squarely at him and smiled back. The Hungarian had the grace to blush. 'I'm glad you feel that way,' he replied, 'but don't let it worry you. I'll be keeping in touch with one or two people here, and they've promised to let me know if you want further help.' He smiled again. 'I'll come back any time I'm needed,' he promised.

The British trio caught the morning express to the capital. Their escort was now reduced to one rather grizzled warrant officer who carried no revolver and who showed an immediate trust in them by going to sleep and awakening only as the train was rushing down the valley towards the outskirts of Buda. They went non-stop through the first of the twin cities, crossed the broad Danube to Pest, glided past the Kir Palota, the palace where the Regent, Admiral Horthy, lived, and stepped out into the bustle and hubbub of the main railway station. It was early afternoon on 14th December, 1943.

The traffic was thicker than they had expected. They crossed the road during a momentary pause and steered the mildly protesting warrant officer into a bar. He couldn't speak English, but he didn't need to. Three or four Hungarian Schnapps, as Dai Davies remarked, would prove the equal of any interpreter, and in any case, the journey was nearly over. The Legation they were visiting was only a couple of blocks away. Why they were going there at all was part of the growing mystery, but both Dai and Joe agreed with Natusch that the ambassador, or plenipotentiary or whoever he was, could wait until they'd washed the travel dust from their throats. Joe sipped his drink appreciatively. 'This is a damn sight better than the Stalag,' he grunted. A well-curved blonde sitting at a table nearby looked up and smiled as she heard the foreign tongue. Joe lifted his glass in salute and smiled back. 'You can include that,' he added. There was understandable emphasis in his voice.

But they didn't dally. The warrant officer, with half-a-dozen schnapps inside him to their three, was still cold sober and aware that time was pressing. He shepherded them outside, called a taxi, and they drove away at express speed. The blonde waved a smiling adieu.

The Legation official seemed a likeable chap. He eyed the three of them, guessed correctly, and turned to the New Zealander. 'Captain Natusch?' he asked. His accent was faultless. 'Glad to see you, Captain. We've been expecting you.' Natusch left Dai and Joe, followed the official into a private office and sat down in the most comfortable chair he'd been in for three years. The Legation man offered a cigarette, poured drinks, and got down to business without delay. 'I believe you've just come from the fortress at Komorom,' he said. He gave the New Zealander a curious look. 'I find it difficult to understand why you were there. It's not too good a place, I believe?'

Natusch couldn't resist a smile. Understatement like this was in the best English tradition. 'Yes, I'm from Komorom,' he agreed. He spoke carefully. 'It was bad when we got there, but conditions improved afterwards. There was, in fact, quite a noticeable change.' A thought struck him. 'You've no more Komoroms in mind, I hope?'

The official shot up his hands in protest. 'No, no!' he said quickly. 'That's all finished now. You're going to a British camp at Szigetvar and you need have no fears. You won't even be detained there, for the good reason that you're not a prisoner.' Raised eyebrows encouraged him. 'The Hungarians,' he went on, 'have treated you British surprisingly well all through the war. There's quite a number of English people here in Budapest, but as far as I know, none of them have had their liberty restricted. Not more than anyone else, that is. The reason is simple. Hungary is not at war with Britain.' He cut short the interruption. 'There has been a declaration of sorts,' he admitted, 'but then there more or less had to be one. It saved Hungary from German occupation.' He waved a hand to dismiss the topic. 'You'll learn fast enough,' he said. 'There'll be plenty of time to discuss politics if you want to, with Colonel Howie. He's expecting you to lunch. Colonel Howie,' he explained briefly, 'is a South African officer who escaped from Germany. He arrived here two months ago.'

Natusch said no more. A Hungarian colonel had motored from Budapest to see him, in company with a Foreign Office man, a Legation had followed up, and now a South African colonel was putting out a lunch invitation. That made three separate and distinct parties, all linked by their common interest in an unknown and unvouched-for British officer. So far, none of the three had bothered to explain where all this was leading, but his mind was at rest. Joe Walker, Dai Davies and he were in Hungary *en route* to the British lines, and these assorted V.I.P.s would need persuasive tongues to deflect them from their purpose.

Dai and Joe stayed at the Legation all day. Just after one o'clock, Natusch was shown into an army staff car and whisked through the streets of Pest to a building near the Houses of Parliament. He climbed a staircase and was met by a clerical gentleman who was expecting him, and who introduced himself as the Very Reverend Alexander Szent-Ivanyi, deputy Bishop of the Unitarian Church of Hungary.

By this time, Natusch was immune to surprise. If the cleric had said that he was the blacksmith from Gretna Green, he would have greeted him as politely and shown as little astonishment; but the Rev. Szent-Ivanyi made up for his cumbersome title with an agreeable brevity. 'I'm glad to see you, Captain,' he said, as they walked into the flat. He spoke with the musical accent of a cultured American, and Natusch wondered fleetingly if there were any educated Hungarians who *didn't* speak English. 'Now let me introduce Colonel Charles Howie. He is anxious to meet you, and I'm sure you'll have plenty to say to him.' He smiled pleasantly and walked towards the door. 'We'll have lunch soon,' he promised.

Colonel Howie turned to Natusch as the door closed. He was a big man in early middle-age, with a military bearing that somehow made his civilian dress seem out of place. 'Glad to see you, Natusch,' he began. He pointed to a settee. 'Sit down and we'll have a chat. First of all, I want you to tell me about yourself, how you got here, where you've come from, what you intend to do – all that sort of thing. And let's have it in full.' His voice was incisive, with something of a sergeant-major's bark to it. It was friendly, for all that, but it didn't make Natusch impatient to confide his secrets. He leaned back comfortably in the settee, offered cigarettes himself, for a change, gave Howie a light, and decided to watch his step. The next few minutes could be tricky. 'It's a long story,' he began, 'so perhaps we'd better skip the first twenty years of it.' He became serious. 'I'm a New Zealander, I was with the Engineers in Greece, was captured at Kalamata in '41, escaped a few times, and landed up eventually in an officers' camp at Bari in Italy.' That was partly true. Natusch had been at Bari, although not in an officers' camp.

Howie nodded. 'Yes,' he prompted. 'And what then?'

Natusch drew on his cigarette and went on with the story. He gave the Colonel a résumé of events since Bari exactly as they'd happened, except that once again he didn't mention the delicate business of rank. Howie listened carefully, interjected a question here and there, tested Natusch's knowledge of military affairs, and mentioned such folk as Brigadier Clifton, Charlie Upham, the New Zealander double V.C., and other members of the New Zealand division. He named some of the Springboks who had visited New Zealand just before the war, but Natusch capped that one fast, and underlined his own *bona fides* in the process, by giving Howie the whole team.

He was very much on home ground here. He'd played Rugby football almost from the day he could walk, and at the time of joining up was reckoned to be one of the fastest three-quarters in the business. The football talk finally convinced Howie of his guest's integrity, and Natusch went on with the yarn, at ease, and with the Colonel now asking questions purely from interest. 'So when the Germans picked me up in the Tarvisio Pass,' the New Zealander concluded, 'I gave my rank as corporal. They didn't question it. Just put me in a Stalag, and from there I went to a working camp. Now I'm here. By the way, I've got two men with me, a sergeant and a private. Both reliable types. I want them to stay with me.' He paused and let the seconds slip by, but the Colonel didn't speak. 'So that's that,' Natusch remarked, an edge of testiness in his voice. 'And now, perhaps, you'll tell me something about yourself and explain your interest in me. You'll understand the curiosity?'

Howie nodded. 'A natural one,' he agreed. His tone was dry. 'I was wondering when you'd ask me that. Well, here's my story, and I'll make it brief.' He lit another cigarette. 'You'll remember Tobruk, naturally. I was captured there in July '42, and was sent to Italy. Camp 48.' A smile appeared. 'I'm no flying three-quarter, or I'd have avoided Italy in general and Campo 48 in particular. From there, I went to Stalag 8B, just after the capitulation. I left Germany altogether last October with a Hungarian Jew named Sanders. You met him at Komorom, so I'm told. So that's that, and here I am, too.' His smile broadened. 'I think we'll agree, Natusch, that private enterprise is best. Eh?'

Natusch nodded. His first impression, that Howie was genuine, and a sound man into the bargain, was strengthened: but he still hadn't said anything about the major issue. The New Zealander waited expectantly, and for perhaps a minute neither of them spoke. It might have been that Howie was making a last test, to sound his nerve, but if he was, it wasn't a hard test. The initiative was his, and Natusch had no intention of taking it from him.

At length the Colonel resumed. 'Well,' he said, 'I'll try to satisfy your curiosity.' The easy tone became suddenly abrupt. 'At the moment, I'm not interested in leaving Hungary. Now that we've met each other, I'm hoping you'll feel that way, too. British soldiers are beginning to get through from the Stalags, and there may be a whole lot of them here quite soon. They'll need someone to look after them. So far, you and I are the only officers who have escaped, so obviously the job's ours. Actually, there's more to it than that – a whole lot more – but what I've said will suffice for the time being.' Colonel Howie spoke deliberately. 'I'll need your help, Natusch. As senior officer, I could insist that you carry out my orders, but I'd prefer you to stay of your own volition. How about it? It could mean more than you think.'

Natusch didn't have to answer right away. The Rev. Szent-Ivanyi appeared at the door, escorted them to the dining-room, and introduced them to a small group of people who were already assembled.

The break afforded time for thought; and Natusch was glad of it. He thought hard. His first loyalty, he reminded himself, was to Dai and Joe, and the assumed captaincy wasn't intended to do more than to ease their passage back to the Desert, where much was afoot, or at least, to Greece. Against that, Howie needed help in something that for all his talk of looking after escaped prisoners, was clearly no ordinary project. He'd said so himself. 'There's more to it than that – a whole lot more.' It sounded interesting. It could be important, too, perhaps more important than getting back to the Desert.

Natusch's brow creased. The mystery, whatever it was, he reflected, certainly didn't lack *dramatis personae*. A War Office, colonels from two armies, a Legation, the deputy bishop of some high church – he'd forgotten its name – were all involved; and no doubt there were even bigger fish swimming around in the shadows. As Howie had said, or at least had inferred, this wasn't a trivial matter.

Natusch's impulse was to say Yes unhesitatingly. With all

this build-up, something big was undoubtedly envisaged, and it sounded very much like cloak-and-dagger work. He was intrigued. He wondered fleetingly what Dai and Joe would make of it all, and especially of his own wavering over their original plan. Maybe, he thought optimistically, they would be just as keen as he was to delve a bit deeper into Howie's proposition. The Colonel hadn't yet disclosed what he wanted done, but from the way he'd spoken, it seemed to offer action and excitement, and if it did, that wouldn't displease either Dai or Joe.

They were halfway through the sweet course before the New Zealander finally decided to join forces with Colonel Howie. A buxom lady on his left seemed pleased when he smiled suddenly, but it wasn't her chatter that prompted the amusement. What was tickling Natusch was the sudden remembrance of a vow he'd made only hours before. The V.I.P.s, he'd decided then, would need to talk fast to change his idea of quitting Hungary at the first opportunity. Well, one of them had done it; but he could thank circumstance rather than a glib tongue for his success.

Natusch didn't regret changing his mind. He hoped very much that his two friends would see it his way and affirm the decision that he had made, *and* not feel that he had let them down: but they were free agents, and would decide for themselves. If either of them disliked the idea, he consoled himself, Howie and his associates should at least be able to make up for the lost rank.

He had only a few more minutes alone with the Colonel before the mystery took a fresh turn. Howie was talking about the British camp at Szigetvar, the place which the Legation officer had mentioned. 'You'll find McLean very helpful,' he summed up. 'He was a top-class escape organizer at the Stalag, and he's a strong character, but I think these chaps at Szigetvar need someone higher than a sergeant-major to handle them. That's why you're going there. I gather there's trouble somewhere. There may have been some friction with Andrassy – I don't know, but I hope not. Count Andrassy—' he explained '—is the local squire. He owns the castle at Szigetvar and all the land for miles around, and of course has a big say in everything that goes on. The camp our chaps are in is inside the castle grounds. *His* castle. You see what I mean? What I want you to do—'

Howie spoke quickly as one or two guests appeared at the door '—is to straighten out any bother you may find there and to make sure that relations between Count Andrassy and the men stay friendly. That's essential. See to it that there's no trouble with the local people, either. I don't care how you do it, but you've got to keep the peace. Understand? I'll back you up all I can.' He looked up as a tall, white-haired man approached. 'And now here's Doctor Ferenc,' he added. 'He wants to talk to you. If you listen hard, it might do your curiosity some good.' Howie smiled and patted Natusch on the shoulder. 'Keep your ears open.'

At first, Natusch thought Dr. Ferenc a crashing bore, despite Howie's over-elaborate build-up The Doctor took him back to the empty dining-room, and for a long time talked about how rough life must have been in the German prison camps, and what a tragedy it was that Hungary had got herself involved in the war. Natusch let him ramble on at his own speed. Some time, possibly within the next hour, the old gentleman was scheduled to say something that would be worth listening to. Until then, there was nothing for it but patience.

Dr. Ferenc came to the point faster than Natusch had expected, although even then it was in a roundabout way. 'It's not long since I was in London myself,' he said. 'I've always advocated a pro-British policy here in Hungary, but of course since the war started, I've had to be circumspect. You'll appreciate that. Still, I hope the time is not too far distant when we can break away from our – er – allies.' Natusch pricked up his ears. Dr. Ferenc, it seemed, was about to get down to business. But it was a false alarm. The doctor had said that he was pro-British, had intimated that some plot was being, or was envisaged, to switch Hungary from the Axis to the Allied side, and it seemed improbable that he'd unburden himself like this unless he was involved, and needed help. Pretty badly. Those last remarks, Natusch reflected, were fairly lethal ones for a Hungarian to make in spy-ridden Budapest.

He felt baffled but exhilarated. Not many private soldiers penetrate to circles where the fate of a nation may be decided. He sat back in his chair and tried to look composed, as if he were used to having this kind of thing happen to him. Inwardly, he was tensed for the doctor's next words –

what he and Howie and Szent-Ivanyi really wanted him to do at Szigetvar, and, if it wasn't too much to ask – why?

But the doctor disappointed him. Instead of getting down to brass tacks, he began telling Natusch about Hungary's history and why she was in the war on the German side and surprisingly, for all the vast impatience to hear more about Szigetvar, the doctor proved interesting.

It was, of course, the most absorbing story in modern politics. Hitler, began Dr. Ferenc, settling himself comfortably in his chair, had been concerned lest the powerful south-eastern bloc of Hungary, Rumania and Yugoslavia should one day turn against him. To counter the potential danger, he decided to split the alliance of the three countries, and in August 1940 he began the process of offering to return to Hungary those provinces in Rumania and Yugoslavia which had been taken from her after the 1918 Armistice. He added a warning that anything less than acceptance would be considered a hostile act against Germany. That cooked Hungary's goose, by aligning her against her own allies. She didn't want her provinces back – not like that – but she knew that refusal would single her out for German occupation, and that Rumania would then be offered a part of Hungary on precisely the same terms. Either way, Hitler held the trump card, and to cut Dr. Ferenc's story short, Hungary accepted.

In March 1941, eight months later, the Fuehrer made his next move. He was now ready to invade Yugoslavia, and he demanded free passage across neutral Hungary for his troops. Once again, Hungary gave in, despite a warning from Britain that if she did, it meant war. The Hungarians didn't want war with Britain any more than Britain did with them, and in point of fact our declaration wasn't made until Stalin reminded Churchill that he'd left this business unfinished. It wasn't, according to Dr. Ferenc, a serious declaration, nor was it meant to be. It came in December 1941, nearly nine months after the British ultimatum had expired, and as yet, neither side had done the other any harm. Allied planes were flying over western Hungary on their bombing raids to Germany, but they weren't harried by Hungarian fighters, nor was any warning sent to the Germans. In return, there were no Allied raids on Budapest, and at night the city wasn't blacked out.

The Doctor smiled. 'So you see, Captain,' he concluded,

'there's no hard feelings between us. We understand what's happened and we haven't returned your declaration of war. That's why British citizens in Hungary are not interned.' The smile vanished suddenly. 'But we are by no means complacent. My friends and I are convinced that Germany will lose the war—' Natusch's eyebrows rose again '—and we don't want the Russian army to occupy our country afterwards. Need I explain why?' The New Zealander said 'No' hastily. If the doctor got on to that subject there'd be no stopping him. But he didn't pursue it. 'This game we play,' he said soberly, 'is a dangerous one. We have to be careful; but we must also be ready to act. The Germans are being forced back, and the time is coming when we shall have to do something to save ourselves from a repetition of the 1918 disaster.'

He leaned forward and gripped Natusch's hand. 'We are counting on your support, Captain. But I do beg you to be careful. Remember the Germans have spies everywhere, and they're on the alert. They may have watched you come into this house, and they may follow you when you leave. If you want to see me again, let me know through Colonel Howie, and I'll arrange a meeting.'

With that, Dr. Ferenc got up, bade Natusch goodbye, and was gone before the New Zealander could ask any of the dozen questions that were on the tip of his tongue. All he knew for certain was that he'd landed feet first into something uncommonly big.

CHAPTER FOUR

THE PLOT UNFOLDS

Colonel Howie came over almost immediately. 'Well, Natusch,' he remarked, 'you've got the layout, eh?' He was bluff and breezy once again, and giving no more away than the Doctor. 'Things are a bit vague at the moment,' he conceded, 'but I'll be seeing you again in a fortnight. By then, I should know something definite. I'll visit you at Szigetvar.' He looked at his watch. 'You'd better go now, or you'll miss your train.' He offered his hand. 'I'm glad I've met you,' he said. 'I think we'll get on well together.'

The army car was still waiting outside. Natusch got in, called at the Legation for Dai Davies and Joe Walker, and reached the railway station with half an hour to spare.

He got time during the journey to Szigetvar to review what had happened at Szent-Ivanyi's flat. His assessment, he felt, was accurate. Howie was working with Ferenc, and also, presumably, with Szent-Ivanyi on this idea of theirs of swinging Hungary over to the Allied side. Obviously, there were higher-ups who knew all about it, and it was just as patent that the Colonel, the Doctor and the Bishop weren't the only lesser lights who were involved. Natusch thought right away of Colonel Utassy, who had visited him at Komorom, and who had no doubt sent his report to either Ferenc or Howie. There were others, too – the Legation chap, Utassy's colleague from the Foreign Office, this Count Andrassy whom he was yet to meet, and more besides. Hell, he thought, this *is* complicated. He'd been brought in to help, but precisely what he had to do hadn't yet been disclosed. It would certainly be something more important – at least he hoped so – than straightening out an alleged spot of bother at Szigetvar, a place he'd never heard of in his life. Natusch shrugged irritably. He was in the conspiracy himself now, but only as a pawn, and things weren't moving fast enough for his liking.

He looked up to see Dai watching him curiously. 'When you're quite ready—' the sergeant began dryly '—remember there's two heads and only one problem.' He saw the frown appearing on Natusch's face, and stiffened slightly. 'O.K., O.K.,' he said. He sounded hurt. 'If you've got to do it the hard way, it's all yours. I'll not interfere. But I had thought we were working together.'

Natusch couldn't say anything just then. The train was crowded and one or two people were already looking up interestedly at the sound of the Welsh voice. He offered a peace cigarette, caught his friend's eye and said one word 'Later.' Fortunately Dai understood.

The journey was a long one. They had to get off the train at a place called Siklos, thirty miles south-east of Szigetvar, and report to the Kommandant of the garrison there, because his authority extended over an area that included both towns. They left the Kommandant next day somewhere about mid-afternoon, but it was another two hours, what with the interminable halts, before they were finished with travelling. Natusch caught a glimpse of a signpost as the train clanked wearily into the station. Szigetvar, it disclosed, was twenty-five kilometres from the Yugoslav border.

Sergeant-Major Norman McLean was on the platform waiting for them. He was a slim, medium-built man, dressed in civilian clothes, and wearing a hat that tilted rakishly over his head in true colonial fashion. Natusch liked his erect bearing, and the determined thrust of his chin. He looked all right, did McLean. If the other men at Szigetvar were anything like him, he decided, there couldn't be much need for a trouble-breaker.

McLean confirmed the feeling. The sergeant-major introduced himself, and they set off for the camp, with Dai and Joe keeping tactfully to the rear, and Natusch already plying the questions that had been intriguing him during the train journey. As yet, he had no inkling of what he was really supposed to do at Szigetvar, but it wouldn't be a bad idea, he felt, if he got to know the lay of the land. 'No, sir,' McLean replied. 'There's no trouble here, at least not in the camp.' The Canadian looked up and smiled. 'Looks like someone's been trying to frighten you, sir. Mind you, I've got a fairly tough bunch of men here, and if you push them, they tend to push back, but I can handle them. Discipline's on the top line.'

They walked on in silence for a moment or two before McLean resumed. 'But I don't get on well with the local police chief,' he went on. 'I have to give him a report on the camp once a week, and we don't hit it off at all. Never have done. That copper hates my guts. But it's mutual. I'm not keen on him, either. He's a big fat chap, full of his own importance, and I think he's upset because I'm not an officer. Reckons it's an affront to his dignity, or something.' McLean spoke contemptuously. 'He's been making the most of it, too. Our boys aren't looking for trouble, but there was a fight with some of the local toughs a few days ago. It didn't amount to much, but old bellyguts was over first thing next morning, medals and all, to slap a curfew on us. I couldn't budge him. Anyone found in the town now after six o'clock'll be arrested on sight.' McLean's voice altered slightly, possibly at the prospect of being able to hand on his dilemma to someone else. 'But it may be different now you're here, sir. Maybe you'll be able to handle him. I sure hope so. The boys don't like being cooped up in the castle. But remember, sir, the old bastard's right touchy about his dignity.'

Natusch smiled to himself at McLean's vehemence and at his confirmation of Tom Sanders' injunction at Komorom. Hungarian officers, it seemed, were more than usually conscious of their status. It was worth remembering. 'Don't worry,' he reassured the Canadian. His smile broke loose. 'I've met some of their top brass already, and I seem to have got on fairly well with them. I'll see your fellow as soon as I can, anyway. And now tell me more about the camp.'

Natusch was intrigued with Count Andrassy's fortress home. It was a huge place, dating from medieval times, and entirely surrounded by a vast wall; but not everything was medieval. They followed the drive from the gatehouse, passed under a sinister-looking archway that no doubt had a portcullis to protect it, and approached a long brick building alive with electric lights blazing from uncurtained windows. From inside came snatches of music and the subdued murmur of voices.

McLean stopped. 'Here we are, sir,' he said. 'We live here. Used to be the stables, but there's been improvements since those days. We had a new bathroom put in about a month ago.' He grinned. 'H. and C., shower, fancy fittings – the lot. You'd think you were in a class hotel.' Natusch looked suitably impressed. The Count, their sponsor, was clearly a generous man. 'The castle's over there,' McLean went on. He pointed into the darkness. 'You'll probably have your quarters there, but you'll have to stay with us until Andrassy gets back. He's gone away for a few days. To Budapest. You can have my room if you wish, sir.'

Natusch was aware, as he stepped through the doorway, that a lot depended on the initial impression that these Szigetvar men got of their new officer. As McLean had said, they were a tough bunch – every one of them had had the courage to escape – and he was prepared for resentment at the sudden and maybe unwelcome intrusion of authority. He had to establish an immediate ascendancy, nevertheless, if he was to merit Colonel Howie's approval. It could be a tricky moment.

He got a pleasant surprise. A score of men looked up as they entered, their gaze shifting quickly from McLean to him, briefly to Dai and Joe, and then back to him. For a few moments he was subjected to an almost clinical scrutiny. At its peak, a big man at the back of the room got up, switched off the radio, and came across. 'Captain Natusch?' he asked. He sounded friendly. 'Glad to see you, sir. We've been expecting you. I'm McGregor. Australian. You're just in time for the news. Like to hear it?'

That seemed to break the ice. Most of the men who had remained seated got to their feet and began milling around, and the few minutes before the B.B.C. commentator's level voice quietened everyone passed in a series of introductions. The majority of men were polite and seemed friendly enough, and as for the minority who withheld their approval, Natusch reminded himself once again that first impressions are often deceptive.

The New Zealander settled down to await Count Andrassy's return from Budapest. McLean gave up his room to him, as promised, and he slept and had his meals apart from the others. He snubbed the few tentative hail-fellow-well-met approaches that were made, partly because he'd never yet seen an officer hobnobbing with his men, and also because he didn't want to get too friendly with anyone at Szigetvar. He had a job to do here, and it seemed essential to maintain the class barrier of a commission. The success of Howie's project might well depend on it.

He made his first move early next morning. Dai Davies went with him to act as German interpreter, and they paid a courtesy visit on the Hungarian chief of police in Szigetvar. After the inevitable formalities were done with, Natusch fired his opening salvo, and with the Komorom strategy firmly in mind, told the police officer that he, a commissioned officer in His Britannic Majesty's armed forces, would henceforth be responsible for keeping order amongst the British personnel at the fortress, and furthermore, that he was to be notified immediately should there be any complaints.

The police chief, a rotund man with several chins, but very different from the ogre that Natusch had been expecting, agreed with surprising readiness. For some reason he seemed anxious to please, and Natusch, puzzled, seized his advantage. 'Tell the officer,' he instructed Dai, 'that from tonight onwards, I intend to allow half my men to remain out until 11 p.m. He will withdraw his arrest order, of course.' That was accepted, too, and the unexpected goodwill showed no sign of being exhausted. 'Tell him that Sergeant-Major McLean and I will enjoy complete freedom of movement,' Natusch continued. 'We may have to leave the castle at any time of the day. Or the night. And that if I do go out, you will accompany me as interpreter. Does he understand that?' The police chief did. He was patently an easy-going character, and it struck Natusch that he must have had some powerful incentive in issuing his arrest-at-sight order. 'He says he's glad you've come here,' Dai interpreted. There was a curious note in his voice. 'If he can help you at any time, all you've got to do is ask him.'

It was a wholly successful interview. The New Zealander felt that for once he had made considerable progress, and he felt better still when Count Andrassy returned that afternoon from Budapest in a gleaming Alfa-Romeo, and sent over an invitation to visit the castle. Natusch accepted, and kept his fingers crossed as McLean conducted him through another archway into the inner part of the fortress. Andrassy, for all he knew, could be playing a major part in this odd drama in which he'd become involved. With his wealth and position, and with escaped British prisoners domiciled inside his castle walls, it seemed unlikely that he could be other than at the nub of it.

The ancestral home of the Andrassy family was an impressive building. It was well preserved, was surrounded by a wide expanse of lawns, and had what appeared to be a mosque at one end. The minaret crowning the mosque still carried an iron crescent, the symbol of the Mohammedan faith. 'That's over four hundred years old,' McLean remarked. 'The Turks captured this place about four centuries ago, and built a mosque to celebrate their victory.' He grinned as they approached the domed building. 'But you needn't worry about putting on your praying slippers. It's a hall now.'

Count Andrassy was waiting. The hall was a comfortable place, and when McLean had completed his introductions and had left them, the two men sat down before an open fire of logs that were burning in what must have been the biggest hearth in Hungary.

Natusch looked at the Count curiously, and with a shade of unease as they waited for refreshments to be brought in. This Hungarian king-of-the-castle wasn't in the least the ascetic type he had been visualizing. Before him sat a stocky, square-headed individual, almost bull-necked, looking more like an all-in wrestler than a leading member of the country's nobility. He didn't look much like a conspirator, either. Natusch watched the broad, honest face opposite him closely and with fast-growing concern as he searched in vain for any comforting trace of guile or duplicity. He found none. His doubts increased disproportionately. This was wrong, he felt. It shouldn't be like this. Andrassy, even if he wasn't the kingpin, was mixed up somewhere in the Budapest plot: and at pretty high level, too. He had to be. Howie had more or less said so. But the man facing him was an innocent, if ever he'd seen one, looked far too open and naïve to be a party to anything devious. And yet here he was, hotfoot from some mysterious business in Budapest, quite possibly with Colonel Howie himself, and with an invitation extended almost at the moment of his return. It didn't make sense. Natusch felt bewilderment creep over him. If his own instant assessment of character turned out to be correct, and the Count was, after all, of no real consequence, why then had he, Roy Natusch, the newly chosen instrument of these too-secretive plotters, been sent to this out-of-the-way place, nearly two hundred miles from the capital?

The New Zealander gave up his self-questioning and speculation, accepted the possible anomaly, and relaxed in his leather chair. He could wait for an explanation. He was, he reflected, cynically becoming inured to waiting. He transferred his interest from Andrassy to the weapons of men long dead which hung on the walls beside and above him, savoured his port and the cigar he'd been given, and waited for the Count to open the proceedings.

They were wholly abortive. 'I am very pleased to welcome you to my home, Captain,' Andrassy began. His English, predictably, was correct and a shade pedantic. 'I hope you will enjoy your stay here.' The Count beamed at his guest. 'I believe you are from New Zealand. It happens that I, too, have been in your country.'

Andrassy's opening gambit established an instant pattern of anecdote and trivia that went on unchecked for an hour. Natusch, inwardly on the *qui vive*, watched and waited in vain for the vital chance remark which would reveal the true purpose of the meeting, and responded politely to the burly Count's conversation. He learnt nothing. Nothing at all, except one fact that became increasingly certain as the afternoon went by. Count Andrassy knew nothing of what was going on behind the scenes, claimed no part in Howie's machinations. Their meeting was a waste of time, an agreeable but wholly futile social exercise.

But presently, despite his disappointment, Natusch found himself warming to the personality of this rugged Hungarian aristocrat. They discussed the war, argued mildly over its probable course, found themselves in agreement on various aspects of military strategy and diplomacy, and had several drinks on the strength of a newly discovered amity. They lit fresh cigars, dismissed the war, and Natusch leaned back as Andrassy told him about the quarters he'd had prepared for his guest, disclosed that his grandfather had been Prime Minister of Hungary, and enthused over his Alfa-Romeo.

The Alfa-Romeo kept them going through two more

drinks and another cigar. In the end, the Count got up. 'I'll show you to your rooms now,' he said amiably. 'And remember – if there's anything you want, tell me, and I'll have it seen to right away.' With that, they strolled out of the mosque into the forecourt. The New Zealander thought fleetingly of prisons and prison-camps, of their squalor and discomfort, and once again blessed Dai Davies for his splendid idea about the captaincy.

His new quarters were as comfortable as the Count had promised. He had a furnished bed-sitting-room, with bookcase, wine cupboards, and – important in the cold winter – a fireplace with an ample supply of logs stacked neatly on either side. Andrassy opened a door. 'Your bathroom,' he beamed. 'D'you like it?' Natusch did. It was a showplace of a bathroom, a newly installed up-to-the-minute job, with a tiled bath and a mass of chrome fittings that Andrassy hastened to manipulate and explain. 'And now,' he continued, pleased at the impression he'd made, 'if you'd care for it, there's just time for a stroll around the ramparts before it grows dark.'

The tour of the castle walls was perhaps the best item of all. They were fifty feet high in parts, the Count said, and no less than forty feet thick at their solid base. They had withstood medieval siege guns, and looked strong enough even now to defy modern artillery. The two men walked on. There were three entrances to the fortress, each at one time guarded by a drawbridge with an enormous portcullis, but the centuries had taken their toll. All three portcullises had gone, and at the north-west corner of the ramparts, Natusch noticed that the foundations had sunk slightly, and that the wall itself was much lower here than elsewhere. He looked over the edge and glanced down. At this point he was barely thirty feet from the ground. His mind noted the fact subconsciously.

Natusch left the Count just before dark and went back to the main camp in high spirits. He had several ideas in mind, and he wanted to broach some of them without delay. The immediate problem of keeping contact with Dai and Joe had been the least difficult to solve. Private Walker, he'd told Andrassy, would be his batman, which would suit Joe, and as interpreter, he'd already nominated Sergeant Dai Davies from a short-list of one: but he wasn't over-elated at having kept his friends close to him. That had been easy, too easy to warrant getting excited about. What was now putting the spring back into his step was knowing that in little more than a day, he'd got himself accepted by the men of the camp, had gained the support of the local police chief, and above all, had won the confidence of the top man in Szigetvar: in short, that he'd already successfully accomplished Colonel Howie's first task.

The next move now belonged to the Rev. Szent-Ivanyi, to Dr. Ferenc, to Colonel Howie himself, and to the anonymous higher-ups who were sponsoring them. If these folk were serious in their attempt to switch Hungary's allegiance, and intended to act as well as talk, he'd give them all the support he was capable of. If the whole business turned out to be talk after all, and no more than that, well, Szigetvar was a mere twenty-five kilometres from the Yugoslav border. He and Dai and Joe could walk that far in one night without difficulty.

Natusch shrugged his shoulders. He could do better than that, he decided. By the time the big decision came, he'd be ready, if it went that way, to lead the whole camp into Yugoslavia – if the camp wanted to accompany him – and once there, they could either work their way south and cross the Adriatic to Italy, or if opportunity offered, join one of the Partisan bands who were harrying the Germans. The prospects were good whatever happened: in the meantime, there was work to do.

He called the men together a few minutes after he reached their billets. 'I've been able to fix one or two things today,' he told them. 'First of all, this curfew order's cancelled—' the few men who were being inattentive pricked their ears up suddenly '—and I've arranged for half of you to stay out each night until eleven o'clock. Including tonight. This,' he emphasized, 'is a concession. From the local police chief. You know what he's like, so I don't need to remind you that if there's any more fighting, and he gets to know about it, we'll probably have the curfew back again: and next time, I may not be able to get it shifted. So steer clear of trouble, all of you. You should know by now that there's a minority pro-Nazi movement in Hungary called the Arrow Cross, and that they're doing all they can to cause trouble. There may be some of these fellows in Szigetvar. If there are, and if they can get this place a bad name – and they'll do their best – it could be closed down. As easy as that.'

Natusch paused whilst his news was digested. 'You are now under full army discipline,' he went on. 'Routine orders will be posted each day, and I shall expect you to read them and to observe them. That is a direct order.' He adopted a slightly milder tone. 'If you have any bother anywhere, come and tell me right away. It's what I'm here for. I'll do all I can to straighten it out. Has anyone any questions?'

No one had. McLean, briefed beforehand, pinned a list of liberty-men to the board the moment Natusch finished speaking, and in the excitement which ensued, those who had awkward questions which could have blunted the edge of the newly delivered *Diktat* forgot to ask them. Natusch, impassive and standing aloof from the crowd, gave the admiring Dai Davies a barely perceptible wink.

There was no more trouble after that. The men trooped out each morning to work on the farms and at the mill nearby, and the camp settled down under the new regime with an unexpected docility. The brawling, which the New Zealander soon learnt had been more widespread than he'd been led to believe, ceased, and when the police chief from Szigetvar visited the castle, it was merely to sample Andrassy's Liebfraumilch and to tell Natusch that the town was quieter now than it had been for months. Nor did the next few weeks disturb the peace. Christmas came, and brought with it a hard frost, and no Howie. Natusch spent Christmas Day with the Andrassy family and dined better than did any of the friends he'd left in the German Stalag, but Howie's non-arrival stopped it from being a memorable day. The Colonel's promised visit was already overdue, and Natusch had now reached the stage where he was listening continually for the noise of a car. He was new to cloak-and-dagger work, and the suspense inseparable from it was proving an unnerving business.

He had to restrain his impatience for another six days, until New Year's Eve, 1943, when the Colonel finally arrived. 'Sorry I'm late, Natusch,' Howie greeted him. He smiled and shook hands warmly. 'I had some business in Budapest that I couldn't leave.' The Colonel lowered his voice. 'Ask me over to your place as soon as we've spent enough time with Andrassy and his friends. I've got some news for you.'

Natusch made the move about an hour later. The conversation flagged a little, and on the plea of arranging camp affairs, he withdrew Howie and himself from the New Year gathering.

The Colonel became brisk and businesslike as soon as he entered Natusch's room. 'We're on the verge of big events,' he began. He appreciatively sipped the wine which had been poured for him.

'I couldn't say much to you at Szent-Ivanyi's – too many people there – but I think you got hold of the general idea. Hungary—' he spoke deliberately '—wants to join the Allies. It is as simple as that. She's been more or less neutral since the war began, and the price she's had to pay for it has been an alliance with Germany. Well, she doesn't think Hitler's going to win this war any more than I do, so now she wants to drop Germany and to negotiate with either Britain or America. At present, she's not sure which of us would do her the most good—' Howie grinned '—which is what's kept me from getting here sooner.' A frown banished the smile. 'I'm pretty heavily mixed up in this business, Natusch. At the moment, we've got an advantage over the Yanks because I'm here and they have to work from outside the country, but there's no knowing how long that will last. You're with me so far?'

Natusch signified that he was, and Howie continued. 'It means we've got to work fast. I'm doing all I can, of course. I contacted London a couple of days ago – I've got a transmitter in Budapest – and I told them how things stand here, that there's a pro-British section of the government, and a pro-American section as well and that both of them are anxious to do a deal. I made it clear that the first Allied envoy who gets here will scoop the pool for his side. You can't say plainer than that.'

Howie drew on his cigarette. He was smiling again. 'For once,' he resumed, 'our politicians have moved fast. I had a reply yesterday to say that a British Mission will be sent here as quickly as possible. The Budapest people have agreed to receive it, and both they and our side have left the arrangements to me. This is where you come in. Our chaps will arrive by parachute, at night-time, of course, but I can't meet them myself. Budapest is stiff with German spies, and they're keeping tabs on pretty well everyone in the scheme. On me, certainly. They don't know who I am yet, and they're not over-concerned, but if I stay here in Szigetvar, or come here often, they'll start making enquiries. That could wreck everything.' He paused again. 'What I want you to do is to signal the plane, collect the Mission fellows when they land, and escort them to the capital. We'll take over from there. I'll provide the transport. Will you do the rest?'

Natusch's mind worked faster then than it had done for a long time. One thing was obvious. He couldn't tell Howie now that he was an impostor, but at this stage of the game it didn't really matter. The Colonel needed help, and a bogus commission would weigh lightly against the difficulties that the practical side of this proposed Mission landing entailed. He was astonished that these problems had been regarded so lightly. It seemed almost unbelievable. British political negotiators, most likely fat and over forty, and making their first real parachute jump, were to leap from a plane at the dead of night, to land at a predetermined spot, and to wait there for him to pick them up and to escort them to their car. Natusch shook his head in disbelief. And just who the hell dreamed this one up, he thought. Those negotiators would more likely need a hearse than a car. They'd be dead lucky if they all landed in one piece and within a mile of the collection point.

He voiced his doubts to Howie. 'Have you got any help laid on for the landing?' he asked. 'Search squads, signals, flares, first-aid, and so on? And suppose some of these chaps break their legs? Or their necks? What then? Have any of them had any experience of parachute jumping?' The Colonel grunted. Perhaps he thought that Natusch was being unduly pessimistic. 'Nothing's laid on,' he said flatly. 'If any of them break their necks, like you say, I suppose those who don't will carry on without them. But nothing's fixed so far. We have to arrange everything at this end – or rather, you have to – and you'll get no official help because the whole job has to be done secretly. You're on your own, Natusch. And it's got to be a night landing way out in the country for fear the Jerries get to know what's happening. My people have insisted on that. It's up to you to iron out the snags. Have you any suggestions?'

Natusch had. He could visualize the scene, and he had suggestions in plenty. He was pleased, too, despite his pessimism and his fear that it might turn out to be a fiasco, that Howie was entrusting the landing to him, and even more that his own hunch that something like this was going to happen had proved right. He allowed himself a brief self-congratulatory smile as he recalled the intensive map-studying which he'd done during the last two weeks. He had backed his hunch, partly to be prepared for just such a contingency as this, and partly because it had also occurred to him that one day, he and his friends, and perhaps the camp with them, might well have to make a sudden dash for freedom. By now, and because of this same diligence, he could pinpoint every road and river between Szigetvar and a point twenty miles inside Yugoslavia. He knew the contours too, and was working hard memorizing the byroads. He wasn't short of ideas.

He got up and produced a map from the bookcase. 'The plane will be coming in from the west,' he said, 'so the pilot shouldn't have much trouble in locating Barc. That's a frontier town on the Drava River, between Hungary and Yugoslavia.' He put a finger on the map. 'There. Once he's over Barc, all the pilot has to do is follow the railroad about forty miles east to Szigetvar.' He warmed to his theme. 'It couldn't be easier. For him, anyway. He'll know the distance, and there's any number of flat places around here that'll do fine for a dropping zone. Some of them are more or less uninhabited.' Howie inspected the map carefully, and nodded agreement. 'We'll need to arrange signals,' Natusch continued. 'Best make them as simple as possible. I think three lights in a straight line with perhaps a red one at the end to show wind direction. We'd better have a code signal, too, to be on the safe side. A torch would do for that.' He grinned. 'You don't want these Mission chaps of yours landing in the middle of Szigetvar.' Howie looked impressed. 'It sounds all right,' he granted. 'Except perhaps as regards locality. We don't want them landing in a bog, either; and there's enough boggy places around here. I'd better arrange for a local chap to help you select the ground. Otherwise everything seems A.1 to me.'

He stretched himself, relieved, apparently, at having successfully delegated this task. 'All we do now then is wait until I get final instructions from London. When I do, I'll either come here myself and give you the codes and so on, or I'll send a message. In the meantime, you stay here. Don't contact me unless it's really imperative, and whatever you do, don't come to Budapest. We don't want German attention focused on either of us. O.K.?'

The Colonel rose from his chair, but Natusch waved him down again. There were two items on his agenda that hadn't been mentioned yet. 'I'll have to enlist two or three of my men almost immediately,' he said. 'I'll need their help to prepare lamps and to do anything else that's wanted. I'll choose them carefully. Is that all right with you?' He had in mind Dai Davies, McLean, and a flight-sergeant named Barrett. 'I'll bring in some more at the last minute.'

Howie made no demur to that suggestion, but looked troubled when Natusch broached the other matter. It was far more important. Some of the men at Szigetvar, he explained, the more perceptive ones, were becoming increasingly uneasy at their continued stay at the castle. They could interpret military and political news better than their colleagues and to them, present omens were anything but comforting. Supposing, they were asking themselves, the Wehrmacht was to forget its non-intervention pact with Hungary and to suddenly invade the country? What then? Wouldn't they go flat out for the internment camps at Szigetvar and elsewhere? And wouldn't they laugh their heads off, as one disgruntled inmate had put it, to find their escapers sitting in a halfway house waiting like a flock of hens for the German fox to reappear? In short, wouldn't it be more sensible to get the hell out of it now, whilst the going was good, and head for Yugoslavia and a more active role than they were pursuing at present?

Natusch finished his report and eyed Howie bleakly. 'I don't blame them,' he said. 'Not a bit. It's what I'd be doing myself if I hadn't met you. So far it's just talk, and no more than that, but I thought I'd better tell you about it. What d'you want me to do?'

Colonel Howie's reply was brief and unambiguous. 'Stop them,' he said flatly. 'At all costs, stop them. This Free Internee arrangement is hanging by a thread as it is. If any of your people leave here now, they'll wreck the whole plan.' He got up and reached for his hat. 'It's up to you, Natusch,' he warned. His voice was suddenly harsh. 'See to it.'

CHAPTER FIVE

FRUSTRATION

JANUARY 1944 passed pleasantly, despite ferocious sub-zero weather which greeted the New Year, and which continued unabated for four weeks. The whole countryside lay suddenly taut and frozen in the grip of winter, and unexpectedly, Natusch found himself granted a relief from tension. Deep snowdrifts and impassable roads stopped the would-be escapers in their tracks, which solved an immediate problem, if only temporarily.

By now, the New Zealander's rank and status had been officially endorsed. The Hungarian government was paying him 300 *pengös* a month, the full rate for a Szados in their regular army, but it was more than he needed, and he used much of the money to purchase equipment for the Mission landing. Dai Davies, Norman McLean and Reg Barrett, now in the secret, worked with him in constructing collapsible shades to hide the glare of the signal lamps. As yet, Natusch hadn't confided in Joe Walker. He trusted Joe, but he'd promised Howie that he wouldn't confide in anyone other than the three N.C.O.s he'd already named. Joe, he decided, would come in later.

February brought with it kinder weather and a promise of better things. On the first day of the new month a messenger arrived with a letter from Colonel Howie. Natusch opened the envelope, saw the code word they'd agreed to use, and read: 'Stand by. Details settled. Will arrive myself or will send a messenger in one week.' There was no signature.

He re-read the message, went over it again from sheer elation, and remembering caution, threw the paper into the fire. He walked to the mirror, beamed at himself, and threw a punch at his image in jubilation. This was *real* news. In a few days, Howie would be here at Szigetvar, the show would be on, it would be action at long last.

The days went by far too slowly. On the seventh, the day Howie was due, another note arrived by the same messenger and Natusch ripped it open with an impatience that this time he didn't try to conceal. 'Cancel previous instruction,' the note read. 'Will communicate later.' It was a terse missive, that in six words knocked the spirit and *élan* right out of the New Zealander. He recovered, dismissed the messenger, went indoors, and caution once again coming to the fore, dropped that letter, too, into the fire.

It was some minutes before Natusch was able to overcome his chagrin and to think constructively. It was obvious that the plotters had suffered a serious setback. Howie wouldn't have cancelled his visit for any less reason, and Natusch wondered if perhaps the Gestapo agents that Dr. Ferenc had warned about so strongly were on to the plot. Maybe, he thought dejectedly, the War Office in London had had second thoughts, and had abandoned the idea as impracticable: but if that were so then there would be no point in making a mystery of it. Howie could at least have given an inkling as to what had happened. A sudden irritation came. The letter had been hand-delivered, but six words make a light burden.

But if disappointment banished excitement, its aftermath brought it back quickly enough, and an element of danger with it. The Szigetvar police chief, now a frequent visitor, and fast developing an educated palate, came unexpectedly to warn Natusch that several plain-clothed Gestapo men had arrived in the town and were asking questions about the British personnel. The New Zealander listened carefully to his visitor, put him at ease with a glass of Andrassy's Liebfraumilch, and did some questioning on his own account. The result was comforting. As yet, the Gestapo had no idea that anything unusual was going on in Szigetvar, and knew no more about proposed parachute landings than did the police chief himself.

As soon as the officer left, Natusch gathered his three henchmen together, told them what had happened, and stressed once again the need for complete security. 'I don't know why the landing's postponed,' he said. 'It could be a small hitch somewhere, but if it is, Howie could have told us.

I wish he had. I don't think the Gestapo have anything to do with it, but they're in Szigetvar right now, so make sure you don't breathe a word. Not even in your sleep.'

Towards the middle of February, more bad news reached the New Zealander when he learnt that the would-be escapers had now made up their minds, and were on the verge of leaving. He reacted vigorously. Howie had again heard from London, and had sent word that the parachute landing *would* be made, despite the postponement, and had stressed that there'd now be a minimum of warning. Natusch remained unconvinced, but the Colonel's news meant that at all costs Szigetvar had to remain open, and that he had to keep his landing team on a short rein: and for all his doubts, Natusch had no intention of failing the Colonel. Some of the intending escapers were in his team, although they didn't know it yet.

The men listened with increasing scepticism as he delivered his ultimatum. 'I believe that some of you chaps are getting fed up staying here at Szigetvar,' he began, 'and that you're thinking of moving off.' The New Zealander ignored the raised eyebrows and questioning looks which greeted his opening remarks. 'I can understand your feelings,' he went on. 'They're natural enough, and if a complication hadn't arisen, I'd support you. All the way. I doubt if I'd have stayed here this long myself, for a start. But I have to impress on you – on all of you – that no one must leave just yet. This is a direct order from me and from Colonel Howie. I'm not at liberty to tell you why we've made it, but you can take it there's a very good reason. The issue at stake is more important—' Natusch paused to allow the inference to sink in '—much more important than the one you have in mind. I must therefore absolutely forbid you to leave Szigetvar. That is all I can say at the moment.'

A confused murmuring of voices went on for over a minute as the men discussed the edict they'd been given, but no one raised a question. Natusch stood unmoved. It would be a highly unpopular order, he knew. He had his doubts, privately, as to whether an officer – any officer – could make demands of his men which seemed so strategically foolish and so morally indefensible, but those doubts didn't assail him. Military etiquette and procedure could be gone into later.

The order, despite an instant and obvious discontent, seemed to have gone over successfully. Natusch waited another minute, decided it had, and was on the point of dismissing the men and inviting McLean and Dai Davies over for a well-deserved Kümmel when a thin, serious-looking man stepped forward. Natusch recognized him immediately. He was Henry Lowenstein, the intellectual of the camp, another Hungarian Jew, who like Tom Sanders had been accepted as a volunteer in the British Army.

The New Zealander was not misled by Lowenstein's nervous manner. Behind it, as he well knew, lay shrewdness and an unusual courage. 'We are concerned at your order, sir,' Henry began. His manner, as always was diffident. 'It seems to place all of us in some danger. But we will obey it nevertheless if—' the word was emphasized '—if you will promise to keep us fully advised about the Germans. Some of us—' he concluded pointedly '—have special reasons for avoiding recapture.'

Natusch, inwardly relieved at this implicit declaration of the camp's trust in him, assented. He smiled at Lowenstein. 'But of course,' he said. 'I give you my word that if I hear of anything that touches on our safety here, I'll let you know that very minute. I'd do this anyway. But I would stress that the danger's not as acute as we seem to have made out. We've been blowing it up a bit. Do remember,' he urged, his smile widening, 'that I live here, too. And I don't like Germans any more than you do. If there's any sign of them coming, you'll need to run hard to keep up with me. But I'll tell you before I go. That's for sure.'

After that, there was no more talk of leaving. The men, their fears and unease relieved by the assurance they had been given, and more so, at Lowenstein's acceptance of it, relaxed, and life at Szigetvar resumed its even tenor. Natusch relaxed, too. He felt almost happy. The men were content, the Mission secret was safe, rumours of invasion were lessening, there wasn't a cloud on the horizon – at least not an unfamiliar cloud. He allowed the tiny voice of caution to go unheard and, unwisely, dropped his guard.

On the last day of February, the Rev. Szent-Ivanyi motored from Budapest to see him. The Mission, Szent-Ivanyi said, was now positively approved and its personnel selected and briefed by the British Foreign Office. They would be parachuting into Hungary within the week. Their plane would follow the railway track from Barc, as Natusch had suggested, drop the parachutists near Szigetvar, and leave him the responsibility for their safe arrival in Budapest. He was to be prepared for action at a moment's notice. Later in the day, Colonel Howie phoned to say that the landing was imminent, and even Andrassy, never an over-observant individual noticed the cheerfulness that the New Zealander was radiating. 'You look pleased, Captain,' he remarked. 'You have won the war?' It was the first time that Natusch had heard the serious Count attempt a joke, and it occurred to him that he might not be too wide of the target at that. He returned the smile. 'It's the spring,' he said. 'It brings big changes.'

That reply also had an element of truth in it, but another phone call next morning rubbed all the vernal good nature out of him. It was from Howie. 'I've another disappointment, I'm afraid,' he said in his clipped voice. 'There's been a hitch. I'll let you know as soon as I hear anything further.' Natusch stood open-mouthed, the flood of protest dammed by sheer astonishment, when a faint click announced that Howie had rung off.

It was about midday before he got his feelings sorted out properly. Howie's curt message had robbed him of his renewed zest, and had almost completely destroyed his ebbing faith in the Mission and in the people with whom he'd been working. But that was silly, he told himself. He tried once again to be reasonable. A project as big and important as the Mission would be bound to face a number of snags before it ever got off the ground. The Allies had everything to gain by it, and as for the Hungarians, they needed Allied help too badly to sabotage any chance they had of getting it.

For them, it was fast becoming a matter of life and death. It was now March 1944, Russian troops were slogging their way through the Carpathians, the Wehrmacht was taking a hammering and slowly retreating, and Hungary lay more or less helpless in the path of the combatants. Unless Providence intervened, and smartly at that, the Hungarians inevitably faced a shambles of blood, destruction, rape and all the rest. No, Natusch decided, their politicians wouldn't wreck the Mission Plan. The same applied to Colonel Howie, only more emphatically. His sole purpose in staying in Hungary was to swing the country over to the Allied side. Right now, Natusch reflected, the Colonel was probably feeling even bluer than he did himself.

But the landing *had* been put off, for all that, and it was the second time it had happened. Natusch found himself suddenly disbelieving all he'd just told himself, and swinging over to the other extreme. Had he given too much thought to this blow-hot, blow-cold plan, he wondered, and too little to the safety of the men at Szigetvar? And this despite the promise he'd made them? Suppose the Wehrmacht did decide to occupy Hungary? Natusch shuddered. But the Germans were bound to invade if the Russian advance continued: and when they did, one of the first things they'd do, as he and everyone else were agreed, would be to take over the internment camps. The thought chilled him. Here he was, a bogus officer in charge of nearly thirty men who had complete trust in him, and for all he knew, he could even now be jeopardizing their safety.

The idea prompted him to move fast. He rang for Joe Walker, his batman, reflecting as he did that if he wanted to, Joe could tell him to go to Hell any time he liked. 'Nip over to the billets, Joe,' he instructed. 'Find Henry Lowenstein and get him over here as quick as you can.' Henry, Natusch felt, was the man to solve this problem.

Lowenstein came up to expectations. 'Yes, sir,' he said. 'The Partisans have contacts pretty well everywhere. There's one living about three miles from here. I know him quite well.'

Natusch put the jackpot question. 'This fellow – will he take us to his friends in Yugoslavia, if it's necessary?' He stressed the last three words.

Lowenstein nodded. 'I think so,' he agreed. 'I'll have to ask him, of course.' Then, directly, 'Why, sir? Has anything happened?'

Natusch didn't beat about the bush. 'No, nothing's happened yet,' he said, 'but we may have to leave here quickly, after all. If we do, it's up to me to see that we get away without any panic, and to know where we're going. If we have your friend on tap to show us where these Partisans hang out, it'll be that much easier. That's all.'

Lowenstein nodded again. He could see that Natusch

didn't intend to unburden himself further. 'Yes, sir,' he said. 'I'll go now.'

He was back before dark. His contact had been at home – Natusch felt that that much luck was owing to him – and he was willing to do everything that Lowenstein had asked. 'He says any time you like, sir,' Henry concluded. 'And the sooner the better. He'll come with us all the way, too. It's about fifty miles.'

That little speech made the purest music in Natusch's ears. An officer, even a self-appointed one, has a conscience of sorts, and during Henry's absence, his had been working overtime. He'd forbidden the men to escape from Szigetvar, lest it should draw attention to the place and so imperil the Mission, and he'd invoked his own and Howie's authority to enforce the ban. They were playing for a bigger stake than the continued liberty of thirty men, or even three thousand men, but if they were to lose on the major issue and the Szigetvar chaps got captured into the bargain – Hell's teeth, Natusch gritted – that'll take some explaining at the court-martial. But it was all right now. If the invasion lights were to flash, a couple of nights' forced marching would see every man in the Szigetvar camp deep into Partisan territory. He didn't know yet whether he'd be with them or not. What he *did* know was that while so much as a flicker of hope remained that the long-delayed parachutists would arrive, they'd find him ready and waiting for them, invasion or no invasion.

He discussed the problem with Szent-Ivanyi that evening. The clergyman knew no more than he did, but it helped them both to let off steam. 'If these chaps don't come soon,' Natusch insisted, 'it'll be too late. The Germans'll be here before them.' He felt a sudden resentment of the whole business. 'You've no idea what happened?'

The clergyman spread his hands. 'No, Captain,' he said. 'None at all. We were warned that a British Mission would be flown in, either tonight or tomorrow night, and we were asked to stand by for final instructions. That's why we telephoned you. Then everything was cancelled. Suddenly.' He gestured again. 'I don't know why. None of us do. But there is still time.'

Natusch felt a bit sour about that, too. 'Don't be so sure,' he warned. 'You Hungarians are inclined to be over-optimistic. The balloon could go up at any time now, and if it does, it'll take most of you by surprise.' He reached back a few days. 'A couple of your Foreign Office chaps called here last week,' he went on. 'They were telling me that the Jerries'll stay on their side of the border for ever. They're wrong, y'know. As soon as the Russians get anywhere near this country, you'll have German troops in Budapest. And here. And everywhere else. You mark my words.'

Szent-Ivanyi nodded. 'I'm inclined to agree with you,' he said. 'The Germans are our allies, or they're supposed to be, but they'd have occupied Hungary long ago if we hadn't made it clear that we'd resist. And kept our armoured divisions ready for them, too.' He smiled faintly. 'By the way,' he went on, 'I already knew you'd had visitors.'

It was Natusch's turn to look surprised. The two Foreign Office men he had mentioned had arrived from nowhere, had stayed a mere half-hour, and had left him none the wiser for their visit: but Szent-Ivanyi apparently knew all about it. If there was precious little action in this drama, there were certainly enough goings-on behind the scenes. 'But they didn't say anything worth listening to,' he protested. 'What did they come for?'

The cleric's eyes twinkled. 'They're connected with us,' he explained. 'When the British emissaries arrive, those men will accompany you to Budapest. They're to act as escorts. They were making themselves familiar with the neighbourhood and checking one or two things. They called on you just to have a look at you.'

That solved one minor mystery, but it didn't shed any worthwhile light on the general scene. Natusch dismissed the Foreign Office men, and mentioned a subject he'd been pondering over ever since Howie's last phone call. 'Have you ever considered—' he asked '—scrapping this parachute business, and sending some of your people to London instead? If they went there, they would contact our government direct, and get something definite arranged. We'd know where we were then.'

Szent-Ivanyi was shaking his head. 'No, no,' he said emphatically. 'It wouldn't work, Captain. The Germans would know long before our people got to London, and that would be the finish of us. We'd get our invasion inside forty-eight hours. If we sent anyone, they'd have no country to come back to.'

Natusch fired his second shot. 'How about Colonel Howie,

then?' he suggested. 'Couldn't he go?' There were more headshakes. 'No, he can't leave Budapest, either,' Szent-Ivanyi replied. 'There are various reasons why, all of them important. For a start ...'

They didn't pursue the reasons. They didn't have time, as the phone rang at that moment, and Natusch's heart leapt as he heard the familiar crisp voice. 'No, there's no news,' it said, 'but I'm sending a messenger to you. He'll give you an address. I want you to memorize it carefully, and if the occasion should arise—' Howie paused '—go to this address and wait for me. If any news comes through, I'll let you know immediately.'

He rang off, but this time he left the New Zealander in a different frame of mind. If the Germans were to invade, Howie had said in effect, he was to go to some place in Budapest to meet him. It was clear, then, that he still had a plan of action, and now that the various loose ends at Szigetvar were securely tied, the knowledge was satisfying. If the Huns did come, the Szigetvar men could use what was tantamount to a safe conduct to the Partisans, and he could go hot-foot to Howie. Maybe that way they'd get something done at last.

But the intrigues that seemed to be an essential part of Hungarian life were by no means over. Colonel Howie's messenger arrived next day with the promised address, and an assurance that if invasion was threatened, Natusch would get a warning either from him, or from the Colonel himself, or perhaps from both of them. The day afterwards, the Rev. Szent-Ivanyi went back to Budapest, and the much-frustrated New Zealander met Baron Biedermann for the first time.

The amiable police chief introduced them. 'Someone here wants to see you,' he said over the phone, and from the deferential way in which he spoke, Natusch gathered that his 'someone' was no ordinary visitor. He made fast time to the town, wondering whether the liqueur-loving police chief was also in the Mission Conspiracy, and if so, how many more people shared the alleged secret.

The tall stranger in civilian dress didn't put an end to his suspense for a good ten minutes. A characteristic of Hungarians is their aversion to going straight to the point, and the three of them sat down, drank coffee, chatted in German about war and weather and back to war, as Natusch tried to stifle his impatience.

Eventually the Baron pushed the idle chatter to one side, and switched abruptly to English that was of the impeccable standard to which Natusch had grown accustomed. 'My wife and I have heard a good deal about you, Captain,' he said. 'We'd like you to spend a day with us at our home.' He paused, fearing perhaps lest he had made it sound a little too casual. 'I've come from Budapest to see you,' he explained carefully. 'I do hope you will accept this special invitation.'

Natusch could hardly say 'No' to so pressing a summons. He promised to visit the Baron in a couple of days' time, bade him *au revoir*, and back once again at the fortress, gave this new mystery to Dai Davies and Norman McLean and let them mull over it. He had, he considered, done his share of solving riddles.

The verdict came fairly quickly, although not before his henchmen had called in Reg Barrett. 'We can't see that it'll do any harm if you go,' Dai summed up. There was a frown on his face. 'We don't think this Baron chap knows about the Mission or he'd have dropped you a hint. In any case, that clergyman pal of yours was here only yesterday, and there doesn't seem to be any tie-up between the two of them.' Dai stroked his chin in perplexity. 'It beats us,' he admitted. 'You'd better go and find out what he wants.'

Natusch called at the Baron's home the next day. It was a big house, set in spacious grounds that even in the depth of winter were neat and well cared for. A servant ushered him into a vast hall, and he waited there, at ease, prepared this time for the dilly-dally and procrastination that would inevitably precede any getting down to business.

The Baron's wife greeted him. She swept regally into the hall, shook hands, said 'I *am* glad to see you, Captain,' in a way that made him feel she really meant it, and led the way into the drawing-room. Natusch was impressed by the size of this room, too, and also by the attractiveness and friendly manner of his hostess. She, too, seemed to have adopted English as her second language. The Baron had chosen well. He entered the room a minute or two later, apologized cheerfully for being late, and began pouring drinks.

The afternoon passed easily, and ended with Natusch feeling that this unhurried way of life had its good points after all. They dined, began discussing the old favourites, war and weather, but soon left them for more interesting topics. He enjoyed himself. The Baron and his wife made agreeable company, showed interest in the views of someone from the other side of the world, and in the end introduced the main theme themselves. 'We're glad you were able to come here so soon,' the Baron said. 'We've enjoyed your company, but what I have to say now is highly confidential. May I take it that you will respect our confidence?' He smiled faintly as Natusch nodded assent. 'I shouldn't have asked you here if I'd been doubtful about that,' he said dryly. He glanced at his wife. 'We've been making enquiries for some time now, and we feel that we can rely on your discretion.'

Natusch nodded again. With this elaborate build-up, something big should be in the offing, and a nod seemed a good neutral gesture. 'I will speak frankly, Captain,' the Baron went on. 'I have been asked by a Minister of our Government to contact you and other reliable Allied officers about a project we have in mind. It is a serious one. As you may know, German pressure is being exerted on Hungary to force her to declare war on the Allies.' He smiled wryly. 'You will recall that England and America declared war on us two years ago, but we haven't yet returned the compliment. We don't want to, either. This doesn't suit the Germans, and what we fear, and indeed have a good reason to believe will happen, is that if we don't declare war against you very soon – within a week or so anyway – they will invade us. We'd resist, or at last I hope we would, and you know yourself what that would mean – air-raids, destruction, everything.'

He paused long enough for Natusch to interject, 'Do you intend to declare war on us?' and answered the question without hesitation. 'No,' he said. 'We do not.' He spoke decisively. 'Germany will lose this war – nothing is more certain – and we're not going to be dragged down with her if we can help it. We must therefore make some gesture to convince the Allies that we have been unwilling partners of the Nazis. That is my Minister's view and my wife and I agree with him.' His voice grew suddenly brisk. 'This is our plan. At the moment there are thousands of ex-prisoners of war, mostly of Slav origin, in Hungary. We want to concentrate them in a number of camps near our border with Yugoslavia.' He glanced up. 'You have the idea? If the Germans invade, these camps will be thrown open, and the ex-prisoners will cross the frontier into Yugoslavia. That way they will retain their liberty and swell the Partisan forces, and we will gain at least a measure of understanding from the Allies. Do I make myself clear?'

Natusch signfied that he did. It wasn't hard to understand *this* plan. It was a good one, and on the face of it could harm no one but the Germans – and the Hungarians – but he withheld the approval that the Baron was anxiously awaiting. There were several points that his host hadn't mentioned, and on his side, one that he didn't intend to mention. 'It's a good idea,' he said eventually. 'But tell me this. Will your people help these prisoners?'

The Baron's answer came readily. 'Yes,' he said, 'of course.'

'With arms?'

'Yes, with arms. And guides.'

Natusch leaned forward, impressed. 'And where do I come in?'

Baron Biedermann sat back and glanced again at his wife. He seemed to draw strength from her presence. 'We want you,' he said unemotionally, 'to take over these camps and to see that they're run properly. If you're there, you can enforce military discipline, ensure that guards are mounted, and so on. We hope to enlist other officers, of course, to share the burden. You will appreciate that if the Germans do invade, they won't give advance warning. That means that if the camps are run in a slovenly fashion, a single company of Fallschirm troops will probably be enough to capture them and to prevent any escapes. That's what you'll have to guard against.'

The Baron's wife took up the theme. 'There will be rifles and machine-guns available,' she said. She smiled at Natusch as if they were organizing a church bazaar. 'We can arrange for them to be supplied right away – discreetly of course. The camps are very near the border, so even if the Germans do drop parachute troops, you should be able to fight your way to the Yugoslav Partisans. We will arrange for you to pass our border patrols without difficulty.'

Natusch looked at Baroness Biedermann in admiration. He liked the delicate way she'd put her proposition, that he and other officers, as yet unnamed and untraced, should command a ragged army several thousands strong, fight off attacks by Nazi parachutists, and guide the rabble into Yugoslavia. He liked, too, the fighting spirit that lay behind the elegance and culture of this woman. If she could find a dozen officers, or even half-a-dozen to equal her own courage and conviction, the mass exodus would probably succeed.

It was a pity, Natusch felt, that he couldn't endorse the plan there and then. His sentiments and inclination were all in favour of a bold constructive move like this, but he wasn't a free agent, which stopped him from giving the Baroness and her husband the encouragement they deserved. His loyalty was to Howie, and he felt fairly certain that the Colonel would regard the whole idea with alarm. And understandably, too. The Baron and the unnamed Minister whom he had said was behind him obviously knew nothing of the existing plan to get Hungary to change sides. If they did, they'd hardly risk inciting a German invasion by planning what were tantamount to mass troop movements. In any case, Natusch asked himself, why was the Baron approaching him instead of going to Howie? The Minister, at least, must know that Colonel Howie was the top British officer in the country.

He did his best to say no as politely as possible. 'I think it's an excellent plan,' he said, 'and if I could, I'd join you now. But you must realize that I have to take my orders from Colonel Howie. He's my direct superior, and I can't do other than keep faith with him. Does he know anything of this?'

The Baroness answered. 'No, Captain,' she said. Natusch sensed the disappointment in her voice. 'You are the first person we have approached. We had Colonel Howie in mind, but we don't know the people he lives with very well, and we didn't care to risk contacting him. You will understand that if either of us visits him in Budapest, or if he comes here, it is bound to attract attention; and German spies are everywhere.' She paused a moment, and then brightened up as an idea occurred to her. 'Perhaps you will visit him yourself and see what he thinks?'

Natusch had been expecting that request, and had already considered it. The answer he knew at once, had to be another 'No'. He couldn't visit Howie just then, partly because he'd been ordered not to, but mainly because if he did, the Mission, from sheer perverseness, would likely arrive whilst he was away. It called for another even more diplomatic refusal than before. 'I'm sorry,' he said. The regret in his voice was genuine. 'I really am, but I can't leave Szigetvar at present, even for a couple of days. I'm afraid you'll have to find some way of contacting him yourself.'

The Baron and his wife were good losers. They recognized the finality in their guest's voice, realized that it was no use pursuing the topic, and promptly dropped it; but no embarrassing hiatus followed. 'Count Andrassy seems very pleased at the way your camp's being run,' the Baron said conversationally. He was at ease, and betrayed no sign of the disappointment he must have been feeling. 'I saw him yesterday. You know, that man has an enormous estate.'

The conversation continued like that, gliding over the awkward places, avoiding reference to what had gone before and was now tacitly forgotten, and in the end, Natusch received another invitation to visit the Baron's home. 'Do come,' he urged. 'We'll be very glad to see you. Both of us.'

The New Zealander would have revisited this very likeable couple had he been able, but this time it was political unrest that interfered with his plans. The pro-Nazi Arrow Cross party, spurred on by rumours of German invasion, suddenly became active. The Arrow Cross, the Hungarian equivalent of Mosley's Fascist Union, was led by a man named Szalasi, and was too weak numerically to constitute a threat, but like its British counterpart, what it lacked in numbers it made up in noise and activity. A local branch, headed by an Austrian, Count Festertich, appeared in Szigetvar and began taking an undue interest in the fortress personnel. Natusch phoned Baron Biedermann whilst the lines were still untapped, suggested that they held over his invitation for a while, and got quick agreement. The Baron knew what was going on. He also phoned Howie and told him, guardedly, that another course of action had been proposed, and as he'd expected, heard it turned down flat. 'Stay where you are, Natusch,' Howie urged. 'You'll be needed. I'm expecting news at any moment now and this time it'll be the real thing. I'll be over myself as soon as it comes through.'

Natusch had to be content with that. He wasn't at all happy at having to stay at Szigetvar, but Howie's intimation, yet once again, of the impending arrival of British envoys left him with no choice. The little group that he controlled was probably least important in the chain between London and Budapest, but the proverb about a chain and its weakest link emphasized how essential it was to the success of the plan. If he and Dai Davies and the others didn't collect the envoys and take them to Budapest, quite clearly neither side would achieve anything, and repercussions of that failure could, without exaggeration, affect the course of the war. But the envoys *would* be collected. Come what may, Natusch decided, he'd be waiting for that plane when it arrived. He could but hope that it would reach Hungary before the Germans did.

Their invasion, if the increasing number of rumours had any basis, was now imminent. The New Zealander would have given a lot to have been able to send Lowenstein to fetch his Partisan friend, and still more to have seen the Szigetvar men setting off for Yugoslavia, but his hands were tied here, too. If the men left now, there would be no one to help him round up missing parachutists, nor could he insure against the possibility of Arrow Cross interference. Again, if he were to send the majority to safety and to keep only those whom he needed, it would still defeat his purpose. Count Festertich or one of his underlings would be burning up the telephone wires to Budapest inside the hour. It was a difficult position to be in, the more so because he couldn't tell the men why they still had to remain at the fortress, despite omens that were now plain to all. It was another item in the sizeable bill that was being presented to Natusch for his 'commission'.

CHAPTER SIX

GESTAPO ALERT

BUT the self-appointed New Zealand captain wasn't the only person with a load of worry on his shoulders. There were others, any number of them. Baron Biedermann and his wife were frustrated at the setback which their recruiting hopes had sustained, Colonel Howie and his friends were on the verge of despair at the way their master plan persisted in misfiring, those members of the Hungarian Foreign Office who were concerned were apprehensive, and no doubt a good many conspirators in other places were sharing the general unease.

Right at the top, with the biggest problem and the heaviest responsibility of all, was Admiral Horthy, Regent of Hungary. He was aware that German suspicion of Hungary's intentions had crystallized, and that the stage was set for a Nazi coup. He knew, too – he had the lessons of Austria, Czechoslovakia, Greece, and other countries to brood over – what that would mean, but at the moment he was powerless to oppose an invasion. His fighting troops were spread out on the western border, guarding it against the Russian threat, and very certainly, no foreign army was interested in helping him. There was but one chance, and that a slim one, as the Admiral realized. If somehow he could confront the massed German forces in the north with his own crack divisions, and make it clear that they would defend their country to the death, and count it a privilege to do so, he might yet win a reprieve. Horthy took a calculated risk. Towards the middle of March 1944, he accepted an invitation from Hitler and went to Berlin, ostensibly to a special conference, and in reality to allow the Hungarian army time to redeploy along their threatened northern frontier. The gamble failed. The Regent arrived in

Berlin, was greeted by the Fuehrer himself, and was being wined and dined by his affable host as the Wehrmacht generals, not far away, completed their final preparations.

The blow fell at dawn on Sunday, 19th March, 1944. German Panzer forces, led by elements of the ill-famed Schutz Staffeln, Hitler's élite Backshirt corps, launched a surprise three-pronged attack on Hungary from Yugoslavia, from Rumania, and from the Reich itself. They swept aside frontier controls, crushed the slight opposition that was offered them, and in three separate columns drove at Budapest. They took over exchange and telegraph communications as they went, effectively silencing all warning of the invasion. Some frenzied telephone calls did get through to the capital, as they were bound to, but the Germans had made the necessary allowances. As early as 6 a.m., S.S. troops already in Budapest changed from plain clothes into uniform, assembled their machine-guns, and seized the nerve centres of the city: and with post offices and telephone exchanges in enemy hands, communications were at once paralysed.

The great majority of the population suspected nothing until 10 a.m. when the first contingent of dusty and travel-stained invaders swept into Budapest, mounting guards at key points as they rushed on. Startled Hungarians in the streets gazed at them in astonishment, and then hurried home to give their families the dire news. Those who lived on the main roads looked down from their windows to see military vehicles full of men in field-grey uniform speeding past. Some shuddered as the first tanks, with their black-clad S.S. crews, rumbled into the city.

There was no opposition. The crack fighting divisions that might have stopped the Huns were still at the Eastern Front, unaware of what was happening, and when they did learn, it was too late. Budapest lay still and quiet under the enemy's heel, her spires and buildings intact and her virtue ravished; but behind the outward façade of peacefulness, a manhunt was already in full swing. Some of the patriots and foreigners marked down on Gestapo blacklists were caught easily, and were taken away with the surprise large on their faces. Others, the wilier ones, had gone to earth. Foremost amongst them was the No. 1 target, Prime Minister Kallay, who stayed hidden in the maze of tunnels under the Castle

Hill, whilst Gestapo agents searched feverishly for him overhead.

The Nazi-controlled press gave banner headlines to the Regent's homecoming, two days later, to the Kir Palota. Admiral Horthy, it announced, had agreed to the occupation of Hungary by German troops, because he was convinced that the move would benefit both countries. A smiling picture of the Regent headed the story to give it credence and authority, and later editions spread a photograph of Hitler and Horthy shaking hands over the full width of their front pages. The German P.R. men believed firmly that if you shout loud enough and long enough people will believe you.

The men at the fortress got none of this news until some time later. At Szigetvar, that Sunday, the first intimation of disaster came as low-flying aircraft roared over the town. Natusch was up and dressed in something under two minutes, and standing on the highest part of the fortress walls before the two minutes became three. He was in time. Above him, Junkers 52 and the bigger Junkers 88 planes were passing over Szigetvar, their wings glistening in the first rays of the sun. There were dozens, scores of them, but above the roar of their engines, the New Zealander heard an even more sinister noise as a road convoy approached from the west. A shiver ran down his back. This was the invasion. It couldn't be anything but invasion, and here, right in the path of it, were he and his men, sitting ducks waiting to be recaptured.

He was turning on his heel, when Reason intervened to quell the feeling of panic. Wait! it ordered. *Was* it invasion? The full-scale job? The planes and approaching convoy were real enough, and were German, without a doubt, but were they *invading* the country? It could be – Reason punched home the point – part of a military exercise, a large-scale troop movement perhaps, maybe even a mock invasion designed to scare the pants off the Hungarians. Who was to know? Was he?

He wasn't, but having stopped to think, he held on a little longer. Colonel Howie and his colleagues in Budapest, he realized, would of necessity have the answer, and if danger really did threaten, one of their first reactions would be – must be – to advise him. They had promised to let him know either by phone or by messenger, or perhaps both, and they would need no prompting to keep their word. The Gestapo had been well represented in Hungary, and might have Natusch's name on the arrest list as well as their own. They would know this. Their safety, therefore, was linked with his, but so far they had shown no awareness of danger, nor sent any warning.

Natusch's appraisal reassured him somewhat, but as the noise of the convoy grew louder, a fresh wave of alarm about his responsibility for the safety of thirty men almost unnerved him. He was sorely tempted to abandon Howie and all his works and to get the hell out of Szigetvar – fast. If he and the men went now, he reminded himself, they would have a fair chance of evading recapture, especially if Lowenstein's friend was still willing to lead the way into Yugoslavia. The journey there would be no harder for the invasion. More likely it would be easier. The troops who had been massed at the border were now spreading out over most of Hungary, which meant that the border would be vulnerable again, and that they'd probably reach the Partisans intact – if they started immediately. One thing was sure. It was now or never.

The New Zealander stood irresolute, almost but not quite decided. What stopped him from flying down the stone steps three at a time was the absence of any message from Budapest. That could have but one meaning – that the 'invasion' *was* a bluff, and that Howie was relying on him not to panic. Natusch knew then where his duty lay. If he were to disband the camp now, it would be a breach of faith on his part, a wavering whilst others stood fast, and the end of any remaining hope of those long-delayed British envoys reaching the Hungarian government. And so much, so very much, depended on the result of that meeting . . .

But it was a big problem for a self-promoted New Zealand sapper to face on his own. Natusch tried to marshal his thoughts more clearly, but the issue remained unchanged – the safety of thirty men, or the success of an intrigue that could shorten the war. He decided to play for the higher stake.

'I'm pretty certain this isn't invasion,' he told the men. 'I've been promised a warning of any real threat, from two sources, both of them reliable, and so far I've heard nothing.

There are no German troops in the town either. I've just checked that. The convoy you saw going past may be on manoeuvres, may be a troop movement – I don't know. I do know this. I'm going into Szigetvar now, and I'll bring you whatever news they've got.' He paused a moment. 'I want you chaps to stay here and not to leave. I must again put that as an order. If there should be any danger, I promise you I'll be right back and we'll be out of this place in about two minutes. Will you accept that?'

Some of the men were jumpy and seemed disinclined to agree, but the New Zealander's stock was high. He now enjoyed the trust of these tough ex-prisoners; but with German planes about, and convoys of armed soldiers only recently in the vicinity, it was a big thing to ask of them. The men stood about uncertainly, their doubt large on their faces, and with their gaze turning slowly to Lowenstein. He, they felt, with more brains than any of them, would know what to do, would have the key to this impasse. Lowenstein kept them waiting as he analysed the present danger. 'O.K., sir,' he said eventually. He spoke slowly, his brow creased in thought. 'There may be something in what you say. We'll wait. But I'll come with you to Szigetvar.'

The police chief knew no more than anyone else, but he had a theory which sounded feasible. 'I don't think they're here to stay,' he said slowly. 'Those tanks and lorries were heading for Budapest, but there's a main road leading south a few kilometres from here. They may have turned off. We don't know yet, but if they have, most likely they're strengthening the frontier between us and Yugoslavia.' He looked at his visitor with a wry smile. 'One day your people may come that way into Hungary. But I've no idea really.' He scratched his head in perplexity. 'We've got no news at all. The phone's been dead all morning.'

That remark electrified Natusch. It was the missing part of the jigsaw puzzle, the key piece, and in those six words the police chief had rid him of nearly all his doubts. His phone wasn't working. If that meant that no phones anywhere were functioning, the invasion was on for certain. The first thing the Germans or any other attackers would do would be to take over communications. He turned to Lowenstein, who had been interpreting for him. 'Let's go, Henry,' he said tersely. 'There's work to do.'

On the way back Natusch made a valiant attempt to get the mystery finally sorted out. It ended with him now feeling about 99 per cent sure that the Germans were going the whole hog, and with absolute certainty missed only by the fact that he'd been promised two warnings, and had had neither. That was inexplicable. Even if the phones were dead, Howie could still have sent his messenger. It made the partial and temporary occupation theories feasible – if only just – and it meant automatically that he himself had to stay at Szigetvar. If either a phone call or a message did get through, it would be sent to him at the fortress, and nowhere else. The Mission could still land, but not unless there was a liaison between it and Howie. He was that liaison.

Natusch's head reeled as he sought for loose ends that might have eluded him. At first he couldn't find any, but there was one more which strengthened the argument against invasion, and he got it as he was on the point of giving up. The Tripartite Pact, he remembered, allowed Germany to move troops along Hungarian roads. They had already done so in preceding months, although not in this area, nor in these numbers. It added strength to the possibility that the Huns weren't yet flat-out.

With that, he ended his exhausting meditation. He'd now got the whole thing in better perspective, although in reality, as he realized full well, he'd solved nothing. The crucial question remained unanswered – was it invasion, or wasn't it – and he knew, as he'd known all along, that there was only one way to find out.

The men were waiting for him at the billets, anxious and keyed up at the danger of once again going behind German barbed wire. Natusch didn't attempt to soothe them. 'I'm sorry, chaps,' he began, 'but I'm no further advanced than when I left here. That's because no one at Szigetvar knows anything, although they're all willing to have a guess. It means that we've got to decide this ourselves. For myself—' he stressed the words '—I don't think the Jerries are in full song yet, but there's a chance I'm wrong. I have your safety to consider, and believe me, I don't want to jeopardize it. At the same time, I'm mixed up in some secret matters, as you will have guessed, and if we clear out now, everything that's at stake will be lost. You understand that?'

The men sensed the urgency and appeal in his voice. One by one, heads nodded in assent.

'Right,' he said briskly, 'we'll stay, but there's no need to court danger. Disperse now, but don't leave Szigetvar. Don't make yourselves too obvious in the town, either. Some of you may have friends there who'll help you to keep off the streets.' He ignored the quick smiles which greeted his suggestion. 'There'll be a roll-call just outside the main gate at two o'clock,' he went on. 'Be there, punctually, because I may have news for you. If the Jerries should get here before two, forget all I've told you and go like steam for the border. I'd recommend side roads. And finally, if any of you want to see me, come any time you like. You'll be welcome. You'll find me in my quarters. Any questions?'

There were no questions, but a too-complete silence indicated the general astonishment. The men were baffled. Their captain had just delivered a homily on the subject of avoiding recapture and almost in the same breath had announced that he was staying inside the fortress. But surely, if the Germans did come, they'd home on the fortress like wasps on a jar of jam? It didn't make sense, except to Natusch, and even to him it was a policy of desperation. What prompted it was the knowledge that he'd had his fill, and more than his fill, of doubt and dither and wishful thinking. He had to bring matters to a head, and get a plain yes or no to the question – did Colonel Howie and the British envoys still need the help he'd been waiting so long to give them? He needed a definite No to that to be his own man again, and staying at the fortress, he reflected grimly, would bring convincing assurance one way or the other very soon. If his own private forecast of events should prove accurate, as seemed probable, it was still worth the risk. He'd been a prisoner before, and Szigetvar is a long way from Germany.

The inaugural two o'clock parade came to nothing. Natusch waited until the last man was safely through the gates, and away from the fortress, and then walked back to his rooms. For the next half-hour he was busy destroying the shades he'd made for the landing lights, and burning letters from Szent-Ivanyi, Howie, Baron Biedermann, the Hungarian Red Cross, the original Legation officer, and various English people in Budapest. The shades were easily replaceable, and weren't much loss. The letters weren't valuable either, or specially incriminating, but he felt that they too would look better as charred ashes, and no doubt their writers would have agreed with him: particularly those who were at all psychic.

When the job was finished, and a check had shown that everything which remained was innocuous, the New Zealander relaxed, sat down in his armchair and picked up *Three Men on the Bummel*. There was nothing else to do, and Jerome K. Jerome isn't a heavy writer. There was no sense, he felt, in meeting trouble halfway.

By now it was almost three o'clock. He read steadily for over an hour, and got quite engrossed. He got up once to stoke the fire and a couple of times for cigarettes and Schnapps, and settled down to a lazy and enjoyable afternoon. At half past four, he was interrupted. A knock sounded, and almost immediately a young German officer walked into the room. Natusch abandoned the Three Men, appropriately enough making a tour of Germany, and rose to his feet. So he was right, after all. The thought occurred, a little tardily perhaps, that there must be less drastic ways than this of appeasing an over-sensitive conscience, but as yet he had no regrets.

'You are the New Zealand captain?' the German asked. Natusch said 'Yes,' and a smile, half-relieved, half-pitying, crossed the young officer's face. 'I have orders to arrest you,' he continued. His English was good, if somewhat laboured. 'You must regard yourself as my prisoner. The other British personnel are already in our hands.'

That remark shook Natusch considerably. Surely none of the men, with the advantage of being in the open, and knowing there were Germans about, had been recaptured? But they had. The officer settled all doubt. 'There are twenty-five,' he said.

Natusch tried bluffing, without much hope of success. 'You can't arrest any of us,' he declared firmly. 'We are already prisoners of the Hungarians. Your ally.'

The German smiled again. This time, he was genuinely amused. 'We do not recognize Hungarian authority,' he explained kindly. 'You are now a German prisoner and subject to German rules. And I must warn you that if you attempt to escape, you will be shot.'

Suddenly abrupt, he clicked his heels, marched out of the room, and was replaced by a Wehrmacht soldier who took up a position by the doorway, and eyed the enemy Hauptsturmfuehrer dispassionately. Natusch gave him one glance, noted the sub-machine gun, and turned back to his book.

But the tough-looking guard didn't hold office for very long. A few minutes later, voices sounded outside the door, and the New Zealander experienced a peculiar sense of dismay as he picked out the two words *Englander* and *Fiend*. *Fiend* means 'spy', and he left Jerome's Three Men there and then to work out their own salvation.

He was sitting in his chair, pretending a nonchalance he didn't feel, as the Gestapo swept into the room. Their leader pointed a finger. 'Natusch?' he snapped. Natusch got up slowly, faced the black-uniformed German, glanced at the swastika on his jacket and at the smooth-shaven face above it and answered him. 'Captain Natusch,' he corrected. 'What d'you want?'

The German didn't reply. Instead, he snapped out a string of orders too fast to follow, although Natusch picked up *Achtung* and *Vorsicht* and heard the word 'Shoot' at least twice. The other Gestapo men nodded obediently, said 'Ja! Ja!' and trooped out – all except a villainous-looking N.C.O. who, replacing the Wehrmacht guard, drew up a chair and sat facing his captive, a Schmeisser automatic pistol laid casually across his knees. Natusch said nothing. It wasn't the time for idle comment. The new man seemed to agree, but he managed a sentence in English, a fragmentary but disconcerting trifle, before he, too, was silent. 'British spy,' he remarked. He pointed, drew a finger significantly across his throat, and grinned. 'Ach! So!' Natusch looked at the bared teeth and narrowed eyes and decided that he could have been spared the sentiment.

But it was a good hint. He got up and went over to the sideboard for a glass of Schnapps to sharpen his wits and help his courage. The Gestapo man didn't move from his chair, nor bat an eyelid, but his Schmeisser kept contact with an easy, almost fluid movement that emphasized that it would have the final word in any argument which might arise. A moment later, morale suffered another setback as the guard leaned over, picked up the glass which Natusch had set down on the table, drained it and eyed him unwinkingly. It was clear that this German had few inhibitions.

The New Zealander still said nothing. The appalling

danger of being in Gestapo hands was beginning to register at last, and he had no time to fret over petty insults. The Geheime Staatspolizei, he reflected, now thoroughly alarmed, had come running on the heels of the military. They knew his name, had put an armed and attentive guard on him, and had given special instructions. It was flattering, but he was in no mood for praise. His arrest could only mean that the Secret Police knew something of the Mission Plan, and it seemed a safe bet that what they didn't know, they'd very soon endeavour to find out. Natusch felt his heart sink. He knew enough to condemn a dozen men – and one woman – and he had no illusions about being able to withhold the knowledge. It became clear then that choice was to be denied him after all. He'd have to make his escape the hard way.

But opportunity was delayed in coming. He left the empty glass on the table, picked up Jerome's comedy once again, and resumed reading; but the studied disinterest didn't work, although he remembered to turn the pages. The N.C.O. remained on the alert, and every now and again another German doing sentry outside the door poked his head in to make sure that all was well. Hopes of using surprise and a Schmeisser automatic to get out of the fortress slowly vanished.

In the end, Natusch put the book down and went to bed, but the Gestapo trusted the night less than they did the day. Each time he awoke, he saw a guard standing about six feet away.

The vigilance didn't relax until the following afternoon. He had a bath in the morning, with a new guard sitting nearby, a revolver in one hand and, surprisingly, a towel in the other. Joe Walker, who had also been recaptured, brought in breakfast, and managed to confirm the claim that the Wehrmacht officer had made the day before. 'They got the lot of us,' Joe whispered, as he set the tray down. 'All except Reg Barrett. He sloped off somewhere.' A cup of coffee appeared at Natusch's elbow. 'Some bastard tipped 'em off,' Joe went on. His voice was a low growl. 'They damn near tore the mill down before they got me, but they knew I was there all right. Yeah, someone squealed. You got any ideas?' Natusch had several ideas, none of them relevant to the 'betrayal', if indeed they had been betrayed, but the guard spotted Joe's lips moving, and his levelled pistol stopped the conversation as it was getting interesting. From then on German orderlies brought in the meals.

After lunch, Natusch waited until the young Wehrmacht officer came in before mentioning that he needed some exercise. The German agreed, but at first Natusch wasn't sure if the request would be granted, because of the immediate argument which developed between the two sets of gaolers. Fortunately, the Wehrmacht officer wasn't a man to be easily intimidated. He silenced the Gestapo squad, gave a brusque all-clear, and a minute or two later Natusch was walking around the castle walls, enjoying the fresh air, and with a new plan slowly developing. A guard followed a few paces behind, stopping when he stopped, keeping a set distance between them, his rifle ready for use.

At a point just over his rooms the New Zealander glanced over the battlements, as if carelessly. It was here that the foundations had sunk and that the wall was at its lowest. He measured the distance to the ground, this time in daylight. It meant a thirty-foot jump to turf that was smooth and had a good deal of 'give' in it. He strolled on, glanced over the wall again once or twice in places that were obviously impossible, the plan growing clearer in his mind.

His two personal guards had now relaxed their original razor keenness, as he knew they must do. The one who patrolled outside his door had discovered that the adjoining room had a log fire in it, and Natusch had made a practice of walking past the other German close enough to be able to hit him before he could shoot or shout. He had something in reserve, too. So far neither of the two guards had discovered that the narrow staircase just outside of his quarters led directly to the roof.

He decided to put the plan into action about an hour after dusk. If he could score a clean knock-out, it would mean that he'd be able to gain the roof unhindered, lower himself over the edge before dropping, and perhaps get away without firing a shot. If things went wrong, he should at least be able to blast a way up the staircase with the Schmeisser, leap from the wall the full thirty feet, and take his chance on the turf being as yielding as he thought it was. Either way, it seemed worth an attempt. Once the Gestapo gained clear ascendancy over the Wehrmacht, there'd be no chance of any kind, nor any further delay in bringing in the unpleasantness.

But the plan went awry. At 4.30 p.m. the young army officer came into the room, accompanied by two of his men and four members of the Gestapo squad. 'We are leaving,' he said. The half-smile that somehow conveyed a touch of sympathy was on his face. 'Transport has been arranged in Szigetvar for you and your men. Will you come now?'

He waited as Natusch put on his coat and packed a few belongings into a suitcase. He made no move to lift the case when it was ready, and the officer, taking his cue, signalled one of the lesser Gestapo lights to carry it. At first, it seemed almost a mutual victory over the hated secret police, but the Army man soon made it clear that he wasn't taking sides. 'Aus!' he snapped. 'Schnell!' And with an escort of seven men, Natusch marched through the doors of the mosque, which had itself witnessed so much strife and disturbance, into the fortress grounds, out to the road beyond, and on to the town. He found the men, Joe Walker amongst them, standing in a square under armed guard. There was no sign of the promised transport.

A few minutes later, an argument began which ended in another victory for the more lenient Army representatives. 'The vehicles are delayed,' the officer observed. He looked calmly at the glowering Gestapo N.C.O. at his side and turned back to Natusch. 'We will wait in the *Gasthaus* until they arrive. But I must first have a parole to cover you and your men. Yes?'

The New Zealander gave the parole without hesitation. It was the least he could do to maintain what still seemed to be a common front against the Gestapo, and he knew in any case that escape was out of the question for another hour and a half. At half past six it would be dark, and opportunities, if there were to be any, would come then. 'We're going into the pub,' he told the men. He waited for the cheers to subside before going on. 'I don't know how long we'll stay there, but I'm giving a parole until half past six. Do as you like after that, but until then, remember, paroles aren't broken.'

Theirs was no exception. The whole group, prisoners and guards alike, trooped into the *Gasthaus*, and very soon lager and Schnapps were being reordered. Natusch kept strictly to

Schnapps, and the fiery liquid never tasted better. Dai Davies and Norman McLean came over, dismissed their own capture in a few words, and began talking agitatedly about his own insecure future. 'They've got you taped,' Dai said urgently. His Welsh accent was very pronounced. 'You've got to get away, man. These Gestapo bastards are itching to turn the heat on. You can see that. Now listen, Roy bach. As soon as this parole's finished you get the hell out of here and keep going, see? We've arranged priority for you, and if we can we'll make some kind of diversion. But remember, you hop it as soon as there's even half a chance.'

Natusch thanked Dai, and assured him and McLean that escape was item number one on his agenda, and that less than half a chance would be welcome. That seemed to satisfy them. They dropped the subject then, by mutal consent, and sat back to enjoy what might well be their last evening together.

At half past six, with every eye watching him, the New Zealander walked over to the young army officer and withdrew the parole. A minute later, despite the immediate increase in vigilance, Sammy Hoare, a New Zealander, sidled down a narrow passage, gained the street and was away. Natusch saw him go, but with several Germans concentrating on him, he wasn't able to use the same road to freedom. Seconds later a guard stationed himself by the passage, possibly by accident, and ruled out any further hope of it proving useful.

The watch tightened as the minutes ticked by. The prisoners remained where they were, continued to chat as if nothing had happened, but everyone sensed the tension that had crept into the air. The door opened suddenly, and those men who had seen Hoare disappear turned sharply; but Sammy hadn't yet made a mistake. Two Wehrmacht soldiers marched in, spoke briefly to the officer, and departed. From where Natusch was seated, he couldn't hear anything of the exchange, but he was soon to learn. Henry Lowenstein, doing his valiant best to hide his agitation, got up and drifted across to Natusch's table. 'I heard them, sir,' he whispered. 'They say there's more S.S. men coming here now. They're taking you away first. By yourself.'

Natusch nodded gratefully to Lowenstein. He was a useful chap to have around. 'Thanks, Henry,' he acknowledged.

'Go back now and keep your ears open. If you hear any more, let's know.'

The New Zealander grew tense as the full significance of Lowenstein's message dawned on him. The Wehrmacht protection, which so far had kept the Gestapo in check, was now running out. It meant that within the hour he might well be facing the most brutal interrogators in Europe, and being asked questions which would sign the death warrants of a dozen men – and one woman. That was – if he arrived at the questioning point.

But the two soldiers were premature. Time dragged by intolerably, making the men apprehensive and irritable and doing the communal morale no good at all. Natusch, in control of his emotions, but with his nerves tautening with the passing minutes, suffered worst. Finally, just before ten o'clock, ears pricked up all around the bar room at the sound of marching feet. They drew nearer and slammed noisily into silence as the command 'Alt!' came just outside the door. A Gestapo Obergefreiter entered, gave the Heil Hitler salute, and spoke briefly to the Wehrmacht officer.

Lowenstein stood at Natusch's side, listening hard. 'This chap's taking you,' he interpreted. 'He's arguing with the other Gestapo now, the ones who've been here all the time. They've got to stay here.' Henry's sentences were coming staccato fashion. 'The new chap says he's got orders to put ten men on you. He's got six outside. Another four are on their way from H.Q. now. It's three kilometres away.' There was a pause, and then Lowenstein turned a shade paler as alarm appeared on his face. 'Watch out! He's coming over!'

Natusch was on his feet before the Gestapo N.C.O. reached his table. He wanted to rob the German of the psychological advantage of singling him out from a crowd, and to make it clear that he wasn't afraid: but a cold feeling in the pit of his stomach was giving the lie point blank to that claim. The German stopped, taken aback apparently at his captive's readiness. He beckoned, ordered 'Kommen sie mit!' in a curt voice, but Natusch beat that ploy, too. He was already moving, although not in the German's direction. He walked across to a group of friends, shook hands with them, went back and said goodbye to Dai Davies, Joe Walker, Norman McLean and Henry Lowenstein, and waved briefly to the rest of the men as he walked out into the night air. The Gestapo N.C.O. followed on his heels.

Six shadows jumped to attention as the two men emerged from the *Gasthaus*. The leading one detached itself from the group, played a torch on Natusch and ran expert hands over his clothes for hidden arms. That done, the S.S. man stepped back.

The Obergefreiter wasted no time. He placed Natusch between the two files of soldiers, glanced briefly around, and gave the command 'March!': and with three guards in front, three behind, and the chief captor at his side, the New Zealander set off along the cobbled streets of Szigetvar towards the as-yet-unnamed inquisitors.

CHAPTER SEVEN

FLIGHT AND PURSUIT

In wartime, life and liberty often depend upon an ability to recognize a crucial moment. If one comes, and is allowed to go by unchallenged, whatever issue is at stake becomes immediately less tangible, less precious, and the inclination to risk everything for it fades: but usually there is a fair warning, or at the least, a warning of sorts. More rarely – much more rarely – a premonition will suggest a solution to an impasse or a hazard, and this time, at the moment when Natusch needed it most of all, one came.

As soon as the squad began marching, his brain shook off the agonizing numbness which had seized it and clicked once again into top gear. There *was* a way out, an extreme one which offered a guarantee of thwarting the Gestapo interrogators – if he chose to take it. He turned thankfully to the Obergefreiter, the relief on his face masked by the darkness. 'Wait,' he said firmly. He delved into a meagre knowledge of German for the right words. 'I have dysentery,' he explained carefully. 'You will allow me to go to the latrine, if you please. Now.' He pointed. 'It is over there.'

For a moment the Obergefreiter stood irresolute, and everything was in the balance. Natusch watched him, taut with suspense. He knew this street intimately, knew every house, every nook and cranny of it. He knew exactly where the latrine was – in a courtyard that was guarded by a pair of huge wooden doors, with opposite, a church almost hidden behind a screen of trees and bushes – and the plan which had leapt into his mind was based on this knowledge. If he could gain a bare five seconds grace – less would do, at a push – the chances of survival and escape were possibly fifty-fifty. The chances of joining the folk already in the churchyard were also even. He shut his eyes to that.

The N.C.O. proved less callous than his predecessor. Possibly he'd had dysentery himself, and knew what it was like at first hand. He hesitated a little longer, thought perhaps of the three kilometres ahead of them, and then waved acquiescence. 'Ja,' he said gruffly. 'Ich verstehe.' He snapped out an order and prisoner and escort crossed the road in a body. The six guards were amused, slightly contemptuous of their captive, and more relaxed because of their contempt. Natusch felt the hair prickling at the back of his neck. The stage was almost set.

The Obergefreiter took no chances. He stationed two of his men in the road, twenty yards apart, left two outside the big wooden doors, and with his torch fixed on his prisoner, accompanied the remaining two guards into the courtyard. Natusch groaned, leaned on the door for support, and as if by accident slammed it shut behind him. That instantly immobilized the four Germans outside, but it was only part of the plan that was now running crystal clear through his mind. He had to go back through those doors. There was no other exit from the courtyard.

The N.C.O. and the inside guards were now on the alert. Natusch walked slowly beneath a low archway towards the centre of the yard, groaned again, and entered the primitive latrine. He came out a few minutes later, said 'Danke' feelingly to the grinning Germans, stepped a few paces ahead of them and waited as they fell in behind. The preliminaries were now over. What would happen next depended on his own fleetness of foot, on the German capacity for quick thinking, and above all, on luck.

They walked back slowly towards the road. Natusch reached the door first, grasped the iron handle, and tugged it open. The men behind stepped back unconsciously, and the New Zealander caught a fleeting glimpse of the two soldiers outside, their rifles slung from their shoulders. There was no time for further reconnaissance. He emerged from the courtyard very fast indeed, his grip already firm on the outside handle of the door. It swung to behind him, and with the crash of heavy timbers echoing in his ears, he flew across the deserted road towards the dark sanctuary of the church grounds.

The S.S. men were well trained. Their reflexes were quick, and the first shot came as Natusch was crashing through the outer bushes of the churchyard. He was perhaps ten yards inside the Stygian darkness when he tripped and fell full length, which was luck with a vengeance. Four rifles barked almost as one, and the bullets whipped over his head. One of them struck the edge of the tombstone above him and hurled sharp splinters of metal and grit into his face. Loud cries of 'Alt!' pursued him, and all the time, increasing in volume, came the angry roars of the three men on the wrong side of the wooden door as they searched frantically for the handle.

Natusch was up again instantly and fleeing like the wind. For a moment or two there was a mad race as one of the guards, forgetting caution in his excitement, pounded after him, but the New Zealander was moving at twice his speed. If the guard or any of his colleagues had been armed with Schmeissers instead of rifles, it would have been a different story – but they hadn't got Schmeissers. Natusch had noted that when they marched away from the *Gasthaus*.

The race didn't last long. The guard tripped, and still bellowing 'Alt!' at the top of his voice, crashed into a ditch. Natusch flew on. He'd got his night vision during the trip to the latrine and could see well enough to avoid obstacles; and with bullets zipping past, mostly wide, but occasionally smacking into the tombstones and the stone angels above them, he reached the far side of the graveyard, emerged on to a road and dashed across towards the protection of a house wall.

He should have made sure, despite the firing, that the road wasn't patrolled, but his luck held. He ran behind the house, whipped off the light-coloured trench coat he was wearing and tucked it under his arm in favour of the darker suit. Across the road he heard feet trampling as the S.S. men searched frantically in the church grounds. They had underestimated his speed, and as yet didn't credit him with a clear start, which was understandable. During the past half-minute, Natusch, with Death at his shoulder reminding him that the location was ideal and that the choice was his, had travelled fast.

A new sound arose as one of the night patrols answered the summons for help. That complicated matters, but no more than the New Zealander had expected. A curfew was in force, which meant that to clear Szigetvar successfully, he'd have to avoid the heavily picketed roads, and that he'd have to travel fast. There were enough Germans in the town to cordon it inside ten minutes, once they got themselves organized.

Fortunately, he was near the extreme northern end of the town. Ahead lay the boundary road, and then a depressing area of marshy ground that stretched outwards for about half a mile. He crossed the road, splashed flat-out through the shallow water, sprinted over the firm ground beyond, and collapsed, temporarily exhausted, at the foot of a railway embankment. But he was fit, and his breath came back fast. He crept up the steep slope, checked this time that there were no patrols, and looked ahead. Fifty yards distant was another road. On it rapidly growing larger, were two pairs of headlamps.

Natusch ran down the reverse side of the embankment at full speed. An Act of Providence, overdue but welcome, saved him from breaking his neck and guarded him as he tore across the pasture land like a demented hare. In his head was the single thought of dodging the cordon, and all tiredness vanished as he flew towards the edge of this new and unexpected highway.

He crouched in the concealment of a ditch as the two army lorries thundered past. One of them stopped two hundred yards further on, but by that time he was running over springy turf towards open country. Behind, diminishing in volume, came shouted commands as the Germans spread out and began cutting off all retreat from Szigetvar. The Gestapo, it seemed, had a high price on his head.

For some minutes after that, the New Zealander ran blindly, concerned only with outflanking and evading any scouts who might have been thrown out from the cordon. That done, he sat down by a tree to rest and to think out a plan of campaign. His freedom, as he well knew, was balanced on a knife edge. A major search would be mounted at dawn, which meant that unless he could find a sanctuary, some place in which to hide, the present liberty would have a short life.

The idea of going to Baron Biedermann's house was pure inspiration. It was, he calculated hastily, about sixteen miles to the north-east, and there were about six hours of darkness left to get there. He rested another five minutes, examined a knee that had been ricked somewhere on route, decided it would have to function willy-nilly, and then set off towards the warmth and shelter that awaited him.

He travelled cross-country throughout the night. Sometimes marshy ground and flooded fields threatened delay, but mostly he was able to keep up a steady pace. He saw no one and no dogs barked; nor was navigation any trouble. Part of the route, the early part, lay directly across the proposed dropping ground of the ill-fated Mission, and crossing it brought a rueful smile to the New Zealander's face. He pressed on into the darkness. In the first light of dawn, with the bare branches of trees already silhouetted against the sky, he walked up the drive that led to the Baron's house. There was no sign of German presence or activity.

He didn't try the front door. It would be barred and bolted, like a front door should be, and Natusch had no intention of rousing servants at this time of the morning: but the house was poorly protected. He found a ground floor window slightly open, pushed it up, and climbed silently into what he recognized as the main drawing-room. He slipped through the heavy curtains and saw a decanter and a tray of glasses sitting invitingly on the sideboard. He poured himself a large whisky, and sat down in the Baron's chair.

He was up again in a couple of minutes. He had no idea where the Baron and his wife slept, but it was essential to find their room and to awaken them before anyone else realized that he was in the house. He had no qualms about invading the bedroom. The danger of being recaptured was too acute for that. He put his glass down, moved over to the door, eased the handle very gently lest it should creak, and got to the next of a series of shocks that were doing their best to turn his hair white. Standing in the passage, massive and imperturbable, was the Baron's butler. In his hands, and pointing straight at him, was a double-barrelled shotgun.

Natusch nearly dropped with shock and astonishment; but the butler, recognizing the intruder, gave a polite 'Gute Morgen.' If he felt surprise, not the flicker of an eyelid betrayed it. It was as if Natusch had called at this unearthly hour by appointment. 'Was machen sie, mein Herr?' he asked.

The New Zealander recovered quickly. It wouldn't do, he felt, to let this phenomenal servant hang on to his advantage, and he countered the question sharply. 'Wo ist Herr Baron Biedermann?' he demanded. 'Schnell, bitte.'

The butler was in no way perturbed. 'The Baron, sir,' he answered unemotionally, 'has gone to Budapest. He is due back tomorrow.'

Natusch repressed his alarm and tried again. 'And the Baroness?'

'The Baroness, sir,' the butler replied, giving an obvious answer, 'is sleeping.'

Natusch turned on him. 'Well wake her, man!' he instructed. 'It is most urgent!' He gestured. 'Lead the way!'

The butler bowed stiffly. 'Ja, mein Herr,' he said. He turned, walked along the corridor, up a flight of stairs that Natusch hadn't seen before, and paused. He was wearing an expression that was very near to doubt. The New Zealander motioned savagely for him to get on with it, and waited in the dim light as the butler tapped discreetly on the bedroom door. His own doubts were rising fast. Would the Baroness help? Or would she – it seemed more probable – refuse to have anything to do with him? It was, after all, only a week or so since he had failed them, had snubbed her and her husband over their own much more practical plan to save the country. She owed him no generosity.

His thoughts were interrupted as the door opened and the Baroness came out, and once again her peculiar spell bewitched him. She was wearing a flowered dressing-gown, and for a moment or two he almost forgot the urgency of his visit. She was svelte and charming, and over twice his age, and yet somehow her unconscious magnetism and vitality banished the conventional barriers. It was a *cri de cœur*, but more of the spirit than the flesh. She beckoned, and with the butler preceding him, Natusch walked into her bedroom and shut the door behind him.

Impassiveness seemed to run in the Baron's family. His wife offered Natusch her hand and regarded him with restrained curiosity. 'Good morning, Captain,' she said politely. 'And what brings you here so early?'

Natusch didn't waste words. 'The Germans are in Szigetvar,' he began. He paused as the Baroness stiffened slightly. 'Don't worry,' he said hastily, reading her thoughts. 'I'm not one of them. They don't know I'm here, either. I escaped from them last night, and no one except you has seen me since then.' The butler, standing behind his mistress, was listening attentively. 'I've come to you,' Natusch went on, 'because there's nobody else I can trust.' He spoke slowly.

'I need help. Badly. I want different clothes, and food, and a chance to rest. My knee has been hurt, too. Will you hide me until tomorrow?'

A wave of exhaustion hit him as he waited for a reply. Quite suddenly he slumped, and but for prompt help from the butler, would have fallen to the floor. It was a purely physical reaction, probably the result of whisky on top of a marathon run, but it touched the Baroness's heart. Natusch came to from the momentary blackout to find himself leaning back in a chair, with the Baroness fretting over him and smoothing his brow. Her hand had a curiously comforting quality. 'Of course you must stay,' she was saying as he opened his eyes. 'You poor man. You're exhausted.' She turned. 'Anton. Bring up hot drinks. Quickly!'

Natusch held up an arresting hand. 'Wait,' he insisted. He looked searchingly at the Baroness, his caution overriding the niceties. 'Is he . . .?'

A half-pitying smile answered him. 'Anton's father and grandfather served our family,' the Baroness reassured him. 'You are safe here.' A hand pressed gently on his shoulder. 'Now lean back and rest.'

All the fight went out of the New Zealander as he obeyed the Baroness's command. He surrendered, fell asleep instantly, and being a sensible woman, she left him to recover from the night's exertions. He slept barely an hour. He was dog-tired and dead weary, but once again, this was no time for inaction. The Baroness, now fully dressed, was standing by him as he opened his eyes. A tray that was giving out a delicious aroma was on a table at her side. She smiled. 'I didn't think you'd sleep long,' she commented. Her hand indicated the laden tray. 'Here is your breakfast. Now eat first, and then when you're ready, you can tell me what happened.'

The meal made a new man of Natusch. The Baroness watched as he demolished bacon and eggs, hot buttered rolls and freshly brewed coffee. She smiled occasionally as he satisfied a tremendous hunger, refusing to listen to a word until eventually he pushed the empty tray to one side. 'Thank you,' he said simply. 'That was wonderful.' He accepted the proffered cigarette, drew heavily on it, and began to retail the night's events.

He summed up. 'It amounts to this,' he said bluntly. 'If I

stay here, you'll be taking a risk. If the Gestapo raid this house, and I'm captured, you may even be shot. And me. And the Baron, too. That's the black side. But there's no reason at all why the Gestapo should come here. They'll hardly be coming for me, anyway. I got away from them last night at a place sixteen miles from here, and they're almost certain to think that I'll be hiding somewhere near Szigetvar. But I'll go if you wish. I would like a change of clothing first, though.' He could see that the Baroness, for all her restraint, was becoming increasingly agitated. His presence was an unfair burden on her in her husband's absence, and her disquiet was largely his own fault for talking so much of danger and firing squads and the like, but he didn't regret it. What he'd said was true, and whilst he needed sanctuary desperately, he couldn't accept it with his benefactress ignorant of the risk she was running.

The Baroness grasped the straw which had been offered. 'It would be better to go,' she said reluctantly. Her self-control was coming back. 'The Gestapo throw a wide net, and as you say, it's a big risk. But I will help you as much as I can. I'll get you some new clothes and then you can take the country tracks to Barc. That's where you want to go, isn't it?' She looked at her guest compassionately, torn between apprehension and pity. 'I'll see Anton now.'

Natusch fell asleep almost before the Baroness left the room. He had an ample breakfast inside him, emphasizing his fatigue, but there was to be little rest for him this day. He awoke, startled, as someone shook him vigorously, managed to focus dulled eyes on the grandfather clock opposite, and realized that barely half an hour had gone by. The Baroness, trembling slightly, but fighting hard for composure, was at his side. 'Wake up, Captain,' she was urging. 'Wake up! The Germans are coming. They're two miles away.'

The last mists of sleep dispersed as Natusch got up. 'Are they searching the houses?' he asked. He breathed again as the Baroness shook her head.

'No, but they're coming this way,' she repeated. 'A patrol of them. Through the woods. I've just been told.'

The New Zealander tried briefly to reassure her. 'But the Germans have invaded your country,' he pointed out. 'They'll be sending out patrols everywhere. It doesn't mean they're suspicious of you.' He moved to the door. 'I'll go now, of course. And believe me, I *am* grateful for your help. And for the clothes, too. I'll put them on.'

A minute or two later Natusch glanced at a mirror to check his appearance. He was astonished at the transformation. The rather precise Szigetvar captain had gone, and in his place stood a villager, slightly unkempt with the day-old beard on his face, dressed in typical peasant garb, with an old cap on his head and a voluminous cloak draped over his shoulders. 'Fine,' he said. 'That's first-class. And now tell me where those Germans are that you were speaking about. I don't want to bump into them.'

The Baroness had obtained detailed information about the patrol. The enemy soldiers, he gathered, were following the route that he had travelled last night, but keeping to the paths. 'You'll have to go back that way if you're going to Barc,' the Baroness advised, 'but there's another path the Germans won't know about.' She drew a diagram. 'Here it is. If you chance to see any of them, all you have to do is drop down and you won't be discovered. But do go, Captain. Go now.' Her nerves were taut. 'Goodbye. And good luck.'

Natusch was already on his way. 'Don't worry,' he called back. 'There's a mist coming up. They'll not get me.' He waved again, and set off for Barc, the frontier town forty miles away, aware that the hurt knee was now stiff and swollen.

He entered the wood at a point which the Baroness had described to him. It began as the little-used track which she had stressed was known only to people who lived in the district, but quite soon it broadened into a distinct path running alongside a stream. He didn't like it. The path was guaranteed to be safe, and the mist was lifting rapidly, but for all that, he went fifty yards or so into the wood and began walking parallel with his original course.

At first it seemed a pointless precaution. He walked on, treading softly and a little painfully under oak and beech trees, came eventually to a clearing in the wood, saw no one, and was halfway across when the alarm bells that were his nerves began jangling. He had veered well away from the stream which was now hidden behind a belt of trees some three or four hundred yards away. Emerging from the trees, dressed in familiar grey-green uniform, was a group of armed soldiers.

Natusch didn't run immediately. Fifty yards distant, on the side remote from the Germans, was another line of trees that offered shelter, but for a few seconds he carried on his set course at the same unhurried speed as before. Inwardly, he was at full gallop. Were these Huns searching for him? For him especially? If so, was there any chance of bluffing them? It would be a risky business trying it, but he had to remember the bad knee. If he were to run, it could let him down at any moment, and it would of course sound the knell of any remote hope of bluffing his way out of this impasse. The line of Germans advanced leisurely, inexorably, cutting down the distance that separated them from the limping villager. Natusch tried frantically to make his decision, but for the second time in two days he was at a loss. His mind raced. The knee was bad, which made flight seem a lunatic idea. Against that, he had no papers, and the peasant disguise was far from perfect. He was fighting off a wave of panic, trying desperately to keep calm, when another soldier appeared from the trees by the stream.

That settled Natusch's dilemma instantly. His brain had barely registered the fact that this man had a field wireless strapped to his back, when despite the stiff knee, he was sprinting like an Olympic champion towards the near wood.

He reached the outer fringe of trees with shouts ringing loud in his ears. He glanced back momentarily to check the enemy tactics and saw the line of soldiers now little more than two hundreds yards away, racing after him. Behind them, standing on the Judas path, was the man with the field radio set. He had one hand clamped to the headphones.

Natusch turned and continued at top speed through the wood. He was running desperately now, aware that this time, more than any other, he was fleeing for his life. These Germans hunting him were under Gestapo orders. That was certain. At two hundred yards, any one of them could have dropped him with ease, but they hadn't fired a shot, and German patrols – certainly all the patrols he'd ever met – were fast men on the trigger. There could be but one reason for it.

He flew on, avoiding pitfalls, leaping fallen trees, alert for the other Germans that he knew must be in the vicinity. The wireless set had told him that much. The pain of the hurt leg went unnoticed as another frightening possibility came to mind. Some of these copses, he remembered, covered hundreds of acres, but others, mere spurs of the larger wood, were barely a quarter of a mile across. There might be no cover.

Seconds later, he got further proof that this day augured badly. He reached the far edge of the wood, cursed it for being too narrow to hide in, ran panting into another clearing, and dug his heels in sharply. Below him, advancing up a slight incline, were more Germans. The cry 'Alt!' rang out instantly.

CHAPTER EIGHT

EVASION

SUDDEN stress affects people in different ways. It robs some of their normal initiative and courage and permits them to do little except stand and gasp until the emergency has registered, or for the most part, is over. Others, the majority of us, are treated in more kindly fashion. We can think and act reasonably quickly, but we aren't blessed with the mental alacrity of those who have reached the top of this particular tree: nor can we ever hope to join them. They are the fortunate few to whom inspiration, often God-sent, gives simultaneously precision appraisal and lightning reflexes; and for the second time in two days, Natusch found himself one of the élite.

There was virtually no chance to hide in the copse. Winter had stripped it of undergrowth, and objects stood out bleakly, but in the inspired moment that came with the cry 'Alt!' he realized that he might yet evade both the German patrols. Behind him, twenty yards back, was a fallen tree. It had no leaves left, it was on the small side, and seemed devoid of all cover. No one would look at it twice. He raced back, bent low, into the copse and covered those twenty yards with about a second to spare. Loud shouts were already ringing through the wood as he dived under the bare branches of the little tree, flicked out the cape so that it enveloped him completely, and lay still, hugging the dead wood, nestling as closely to it as its own bark.

The sound of running feet reached him from the far side of the tree. He raised his head imperceptibly, peered with one eye over the fallen trunk and dimly, through the loose mesh of the cape, saw the first of his pursuers. A young jack-booted German, rifle at the ready, passed about twenty yards away, scanning the trees ahead, looking upwards at the larger ones. Two more soldiers appeared, strung widely apart, and then, from behind him, came the vanguard of the second patrol. Natusch lowered his head and stopped breathing as a dozen Germans ran in different directions through the copse. Probably none of them gave his tree a second glance. The skeleton branches were breaking his outline, the dark cloak was blending perfectly with its background, and he lay as still as death. The camouflage was accidental and superlative.

Shouts sounded again as the Germans reached the edge of the copse and called to their comrades. An excited bellow came from somewhere behind Natusch – far behind – and once again there was a stampede of flying feet; but this time he was secure, with the tree between him and the approaching Huns. One of them, more exuberant than the others, leapt the fallen trunk, landed perhaps a yard from the New Zealander's prone body, and careered away at top speed, leaving promotion behind him.

Gradually, silence replaced the bedlam of shouting and heavy footfalls. Natusch lay still. It was unlikely that the Germans would return, but possible that they'd left one of their number behind as a precautionary measure. If they had, he gave him no help. Anything that moved in this copse would be seen instantly.

The silence broke slowly. Birds resumed their interrupted song, and Natusch listened as they began fluttering in the branches of the little tree. A woodpecker's crack-like hammering startled him, until he realized that it held no menace, and he fell to wondering whether these strange birds ever got headaches. Time went by. A robin perched on a twig a foot or so from his head, eyed him gravely, gained confidence from his stillness, and poured out a song that was full of cheerful assurance. It flew away as peasants' voices and the noise of axes drifted nearer, but in its place came two squirrels who played and leapt through the branches above him.

Dusk was falling before Natusch left the copse where the little tree had done him such yeoman service. He got up, massaged the faithful knee, which seemed to have profited from a ten-hour rest, and limped off along woodland trails in the direction of Szigetvar. He'd given up his original idea of going to Barc, and thence to Yugoslavia. There is a limit to the punishment that a knee can take, and he was already approaching it. It left no option but to return to the one place which above all others held danger for him, but where help was assured. There was John, Natusch reflected, and John was rock steady.

He walked on into the gathering darkness, ignoring the growing pangs of hunger, thinking hard. He wasn't sure that he wanted to go to Barc now, anyway. Nor was there much point at present in trying to contact Henry Lowenstein's Partisan. He had the man's address, but he'd never met him, had never been to his house, and he could hardly go searching for it in daylight. In any case, it was highly unlikely that the Partisan would be at home. He'd know that Lowenstein had been captured, along with the other ex-prisoners, and he'd be well aware that with the Gestapo around, his own best plan by far would be to clear out for a while and see what happened. There was also the hurt knee to consider. It wouldn't stand up to the fifty-mile trek to Partisan territory. It probably wouldn't do five miles, never mind fifty. No, Natusch decided, neither Szigetvar nor Barc seemed to offer much in the way of real help. He abandoned them, and turned once again to the idea that had lain all the time at the back of his mind.

Budapest would be better, he reflected – if he could get there. He'd heard nothing from Colonel Howie now for a fortnight, but he hadn't forgotten the South African officer, nor was he allowing the non-appearance of the promised warnings to rankle. He still trusted this brusque man, despite what had happened, and there would be, he felt, a sufficient explanation of the lapse. He could listen to it – and evaluate it – when he reached Budapest and found Howie. He didn't attribute the inglorious end of the Mission Plan to the South African, either. It, in its turn, was an ambitious and wholly worthwhile project that had never got off the ground – Natusch smiled to himself at his unwitting pun – had never got *down* to the ground. It had been jinxed, had been doomed from the very beginning, and there was no point in trying to pin the blame on anyone in particular.

The Colonel, he felt, was still a good man to follow. He'd be in Budapest now, possibly at the emergency address which the messenger had brought to Szigetvar, and maybe he was already working on some new scheme to harass the Germans. If he was, he'd no doubt be glad to see his right-hand man again; and if he happened to need help – well, Natusch decided, he could hardly refuse to join in just because a few Gestapo thugs were on his trail. The New Zealander chewed reflectively on a blade of grass as he walked along, and looked for some less naïve reason for revisiting Budapest. There was one, of course, the obvious one. If he went there, he should be able to get a false identity card without too much trouble, and Captain Natusch of Szigetvar could then disappear once and for all. That would settle the Gestapo's hash, and would make life a great deal less precarious.

Nor would he be visiting his superior without bearing a gift. His offering would be an escape route to Yugoslavia, and there Howie's interest assumed sizeable proportions. He might yet need a get-away plan urgently, and if he did, once the current hue and cry had died down, Henry Lowenstein's Partisan should be back in business. It would be a poor diplomat who couldn't follow that particular rainbow to its end.

There remained – the New Zealander shook his head vigorously as complications piled in – distances and difficulties to be considered. Budapest, two hundred miles to the north-east, meant a train journey, which in turn called for papers, schedules and other things he hadn't got. There was the language problem, too. He wouldn't even be able to buy a ticket – unless he asked for it in German, which could be risky. Natusch spat out the mangled remains of the grass stalk and gave up. Planning, he decided, could wait until he'd contacted John. Maybe John would have some brainwave that would solve all these quandaries.

He walked all through the night. He had five or six hours longer than on his first trip, and about two miles less to travel, but this time he did no running. He conserved his strength, trod very carefully, and reached the outskirts of Szigetvar just before dawn. It was early, but the margin was a slender one. The people of Szigetvar mostly go to bed before dark, and get up before light, and women were rattling buckets under street corner taps as he reached John's home. There was no sign of the German soldiery.

The New Zealander walked through the arched gateway of the house and knocked quietly on the door. He was tired and ravenously hungry, but for the first time in four days he was feeling at ease. John, a grocer with an unpronounceable surname, was the one man in the town whom he trusted implicitly, whom he knew beyond doubt would stand by him at all times.

He felt relief flood through him as John answered the door, recognized his visitor, and beckoned. The Hungarian took him by the arm, smiling broadly, as if admitting hunted fugitives into his house was an everyday affair, and piloted him to a door at the far side of the room. A man stood up as Natusch entered. John's grin widened as his two guests stared at each other for a moment, nonplussed, faintly alarmed, and then moved forward simultaneously with outstretched hands. 'Reg!' Natusch hailed. 'How the hell did you get here?' The tall man dressed in dungarees and looking very much the peasant he was simulating was Flight-Sergeant Reginald Barrett.

Barrett stopped pumping Natusch's hand. 'I've been here since Sunday,' he replied. His face mirrored his relief. 'I moved in when the Jerries came. It's handy being able to speak the lingo a bit, y'know. John came for me himself. But what happened to you? We heard that the Gestapo had caught you, but they put it out yesterday that you'd been shot.'

Natusch tried to keep a poker face. 'They exaggerated,' he explained. 'But you can give them full marks for trying.' He became serious. 'Look, Reg, I can't stay here long. It's too damn risky. But what about you? What d'you intend to do?'

Barrett's answer was wholly practical. 'Right now,' he said, 'I'm going to have my breakfast. It's almost ready.' He pointed to John, who was again standing at the door, this time coffee pot in hand. 'Care to join me? We'll do the thinking afterwards.'

Natusch enjoyed his breakfast. It was almost a replica of the one he had had twenty-four hours earlier, and was as satisfying. After that, he washed and shaved before they retired to the small bedroom and got down to serious discussion. They agreed immediately that they would have to leave John's house without delay. Barrett, unknown to the Germans, and speaking passable Hungarian, would no doubt survive a house-to-house search – if it came to that – but Natusch's presence was lethal. It placed John at unacceptable risk, the more so because he knew the Gestapo and their methods equally as well as they did.

Barrett accepted Natusch's suggestion without reservation. He had been intending to leave Szigetvar himself, but with no spur of desperation to goad him, and with little idea of where to go or what to do, he had so far dallied. A plan, any plan, was more than welcome. 'Great!' he said enthusiastically. 'We'll go there by train. Today. The Jerries haven't banned rail travel yet, and they're not checking passports.' He grinned. 'Just as well. I haven't got one. But we'll need money for fares and meals and so on, and I haven't got any of that, I gave all I had to John. How are you fixed?'

Natusch produced a sheaf of banknotes that the Gestapo searcher had missed. There were about 500 *pengös*, nearly two months' pay, in the thick roll. He handed it to an astonished Barrett with studied unconcern. 'Take it,' he instructed. 'You'll be buying the tickets, not me. But give John a sub before we go. He deserves the lot.'

The two men left by the back door just after dark and just before the newly imposed curfew came into force, which was the only time to offer a reasonable margin of safety. The Germans now seemed to have accepted that Natusch had won clear of the town, and their vigilance had decreased, but he knew well that if anyone were to recognize him, the news would travel fast and with disastrous result. They avoided the main streets, gave passers-by a wide berth, and gained the comparative safety of open country without incident.

Their plan was clear and precise. Szulok, a small town twelve miles to the west, seemed an obvious starting point for the journey to Budapest. No one in Szulok knew them, and the branch line which served the town went straight to Kaposvar, the main junction for the capital. From there, barring accidents – Natusch crossed his fingers hurriedly – it should be plain sailing.

They reached the outskirts of Szulok somewhere around midnight, again without incident. A deserted hut, about a mile from the town, offered shelter of a kind, and Natusch, with heavy arrears of sleep to make up, welcomed its invitation; but the night was bitterly cold, and an icy wind denied him the rest that his body was now craving. They left the cheerless hut without regret somewhere around nine o'clock next morning, satisfied themselves that the people of Szulok really were up and doing, walked the remaining few hundred yards to the railway station, and sauntered unchallenged past the Wehrmacht sentry at the entrance. Without any warning at all, they ran into the first of a series of new complications.

The familiar painted direction signs which they were expecting to see were missing. In their place, challenging interpretation and defying the uninitiated, were huge timetable sheets posted on the station wall, printed in Hungarian, and complete with all the mysterious ciphers and abbreviations common to railway timetables the world over.

To Natusch, they were incomprehensible. No more, no less. They might just as well have been written in Chinese. He threw in the towel right away, but Barrett was made of sterner stuff. He shut his eyes tight, muttered 'My God!' in a voice just above a whisper, and began decoding.

He succeeded. He discovered what time the train left, confirmed – miraculously, Natusch thought – that it did stop at Kaposvar, and worked out that there would be a mere ten minutes wait there before the Budapest express came thundering in from Zagreb. When Barrett finished, there were deep furrows carved in his brow. 'Hell's bells!' he breathed. 'That was some job! Come on, Roy. I need a drink.'

The waiting-room café sold beer and cognac, but oddly, not food. Barrett lined up in a queue with a number of German soldiers whilst Natusch commandeered a table for two, and brought out what remained of the packet of sandwiches that John had given them. It wasn't much, but it sufficed. They supplemented it with cognac until the last lingering coldness was finally driven out, and then it was only a matter of waiting.

At Kaposvar, they detrained and straight away checked their timetable. It was a wise move which revealed that there was an hour to wait instead of the ten minutes mentioned at Szulok: but the Kaposvar waiting room made it an easy penance. It sold meat pies, beer and picture papers, and as soon as they'd purchased all three, they settled down at a table next to the ubiquitous German soldiery. They were making a point of staying close to the Wehrmacht. The Gestapo had a long arm, and it was good policy to play safe.

The Kaposvar–Budapest journey left little impression upon either Natusch or Barrett. The cumulative effect of tiredness, too much cognac, and the monotonous clicking of train wheels lulled them to sleep almost as soon as it started. The train was packed, but they managed to get seats, and they sat, swaying occasionally to the train's motion, not speaking, content with their uncomfortable respite. They slept bolt upright for six hours, wedged like corks in bottles by the press of people around them, and in some mysterious way won back all their normal alertness and quickness of thought.

At ten o'clock, the express drew up majestically in Budapest station, and the two men, now in the best of spirits, jumped down on to the platform. Natusch, particularly, was elated. He had dodged the Gestapo, had thrown them completely off his trail, and here he was, only a mile or so from Howie and Szent-Ivanyi, ready to don a new identity, and to help, if help were needed, in whatever project had succeeded the Mission Plan. He glanced at the crowd milling at the station exit, turned impatiently to Barrett, who seemed to be hanging back, and urged him to hurry. He whirled around again as a delayed message registered. He almost stopped breathing. The crowd at the platform exit had grown larger. At its head, replacing the railway employees, impeding progress, checking tickets and passengers alike, was a group of uniformed Gestapo.

Barrett had already seen them. 'Quick! Double back along the track!' he hissed. They turned as one man, walked quickly past stragglers who were still getting off the train, reached the end of their own coach, and stopped. At the other end of the platform, hands on their revolver holsters, were two more Gestapo men.

'Let's hide in the carriage,' Natusch suggested desperately, but he knew before the words left his mouth that it was an impracticable suggestion. More Gestapo had appeared on the platform opposite, and in any case, the train would be searched. There was nothing more certain. 'Come on, Reg,' he said. Somehow, in that split second, the feeling of panic had gone. He took Barrett's arm. 'Let's get near the end of the queue. Maybe we can bluff them.'

Some of the nervousness came back as they neared the barrier. There were six Gestapo N.C.O.s there, three on either side, all busy examining passports. Twice, as the impatient crowd surged forward, a man was drawn out and ordered to wait. His papers, they gathered, weren't accurate enough, which made their own outlook a poor one. They had no papers.

The inspiration came in time, as Natusch was praying it would. The Hungarians, unused to German regimentation, were on the verge of getting out of hand, and it occurred to him that given a little extra incitement, the crowd might yet see them out of danger. He nudged Barrett and explained the idea in a few brief whispers.

They held their fire until only a dozen or so people were in front of them. Then, with Barrett's right hand clamped in Natusch's left, and with their arms spanning the full width of the queue, Natusch gave the signal. They heaved with every ounce of their strength, lifted the two men directly in front of them clean off their feet and carried them forward half a dozen paces under their own sheer momentum. Over a dozen men cannoned one into the other, swept forward irresistibly and surged through the barricade in a solid mass. Most of those who were behind had the good sense to follow up fast, which made the manoeuvre twice as effective.

Two of the Germans went down immediately and were trampled on. The others stumbled, regained their balance, and instinctively their hands went for their revolvers; but it was only normal reaction. Not even the Gestapo could shoot innocent bystanders without some excuse – at least not yet in Hungary – and the trigger hands halted, came up empty, and reached out viciously to grab at the men who had overwhelmed them.

But if the Germans were mad, the Hungarians were madder. Some rushed past the German terror police, cursing and shouting at them, whilst others stayed to argue. Natusch and Barrett were in the van of the more discreet section. The New Zealander dodged one of the Gestapo, tripped another who was hurling himself into the fray, and a moment later was pushing a way through excited onlookers towards the exit. Barrett was faster. Natusch found him waiting outside the station, his hair and clothes dishevelled. 'Good show, Roy!' he panted. 'My, but we bowled the bastards over, didn't we?' His grin broadened as a delicious moment came back and was savoured once again. 'I kicked one of them,' the flight-sergeant went on. 'Accidentally, of course. Bang in the earhole.'

CHAPTER NINE

DISASTER STRIKES

A TAXI dropped them in Kohary-utca, the street where the Rev. Szent-Ivanyi had his apartment. Natusch didn't know the number of the house, but a brief reconnaissance brought him to the right door. There was no one about. A bell rang faintly somewhere inside the house, and he gave Barrett a buoyant thumbs-up sign as footsteps sounded in the hall. The night's lodging, with no trouble at all, was solved.

But he was over-optimistic. Szent-Ivanyi was surprised to see them, which was understandable, but he admitted them to the house and got down to business without wasting time. No, he regretted, he didn't know where Colonel Howie was. He hadn't seen him since the Germans had invaded the capital almost a week ago. Nor, he again regretted, could he help them to find a place to stay, but the perilous journey from Szulok wasn't altogether wasted. The cleric led them into his kitchen, made up two neat packets of sandwiches, and extracted some notes from his wallet. 'I wish I could do more,' he said. It was obvious that he meant it. 'You could stay here willingly, but it would be too dangerous. You are taking a risk now. We all are. The Gestapo were here this morning, and someone may be watching.' He paused at the door. 'But if you need more money, or food, come back. I will help you. But be careful.'

That seemed fair enough, and indeed gallant of the Rev. Szent-Ivanyi, and Natusch, down to earth again, decided to leave the question of false passports in abeyance. He had one or two other contacts, the Legation official prominent amongst them, and Szent-Ivanyi had shown enough generosity for one night. But none of this helped with the immediate problem. The two fugitives walked out into the night wondering, not for the first time, what they should do next, and in particular, where they would find a place to sleep.

Natusch, for his part, had a more pressing worry to contend with. His knee, the one he had ricked in his wild flight from the Szigetvar Gestapo, was playing up again, and was now badly swollen. All it needed was rest and perhaps a little medical care for the swelling to subside, but clearly it wouldn't last. But if his knee was bad, his memory was still in good fettle. They walked along Kohary-utca, emerged by the Houses of Parliament, and saw a taxi standing by the kerb. It triggered his mind into activity. 'Come on, Reg,' he said jubilantly. 'I think I've got it.'

The taxi took them across the Danube from Buda and stopped about a quarter of a mile from the Kir Polota in Pest. Natusch paid the driver, and with a puzzled Barrett in tow, set about locating Evelyn Gore-Symes's address. It was around here somewhere, and Evelyn, as he told Barrett, was easily their best prospect. She was an English girl, domiciled in the capital, whom he'd first met two or three months back when she was making a visit to Szigetvar to help the escaped British prisoners. He knew her address exactly, because he'd made a point of remembering addresses, and had two or three more still stored away that might yet prove useful: but Evelyn's, when they eventually found it, was another letdown. They stopped outside the big block of flats and looked at each other, both of them seeking the inspiration that this time refused to come. It was now well after eleven o'clock and only sentinel windows in the tall building remained lit. Natusch shook his head. 'We can't knock her up now,' he decided reluctantly. 'It's too late. I doubt if she could fix us up tonight anyway. But here it is, Reg.' He tried to sound cheerful. 'Tomorrow, there'll be a hot dinner for you. Right here.'

The night that preceded the promised hot dinner was one of the most unpleasant either man had yet experienced. The church, lower down the road, was locked and hopes of a comfortable pew vanished abruptly: but some construction work was going on, and the vaults below the church were open. Natusch and Barrett crept around to the back of the building, picked a way through a medley of tombstones and builders' materials and climbed down into a newly concreted vault. A graveyard chill bit into them before they'd been there two minutes, but they had to put up with it as best they could. There was nowhere else to go. They found a couple of ten-inch planks, rested them on bricks, balanced themselves precariously on the makeshift beds, and somehow stayed balanced through the long weary night. The cold grew intense in the small hours and sleep came fitfully. They would have been more comfortable in a Gestapo cell.

The next morning was warm and sunny, as if it were trying to make amends for their discomfort, but they were still shivering as they again approached the tall building where Evelyn Gore-Symes lived.

Evelyn, even more surprised than Szent-Ivanyi, greeted Natusch with open arms. She was an attractive girl in her early twenties, an Embassy secretary, with a neat figure, auburn hair and an unusual fund of common sense. An instinctive friendship had developed between them although they had met only two or three times, but the pressure of events had so far kept it on a platonic basis. In real war, as opposed to its fictional counterpart, there is little scope for romantic inclination, and when they had said an appropriate 'Hello' and Reg Barrett had been introduced, Natusch contented himself with a brief résumé of events. He said nothing about the graveyard vault, did mention that his knee would appreciate some attention, and gave an immediate Yes to Evelyn's more practical suggestion. About ten minutes later, he and Barrett were sitting down to a traditional English breakfast.

As soon as the dishes were cleared away, Evelyn produced a medical case and a footstool, and when all was finished, the much-abused knee was neatly bound in gauze and bandage, and already feeling a great deal better.

It wasn't until then that the real conversation began. 'No,' Evelyn replied. 'I've no idea where Colonel Howie is. People aren't found easily these days, you know. What do you want him for?'

Natusch smiled. 'Just to see him,' he said evasively. 'Old times' sake, I suppose. We met a few times before the Jerries got here. Now they've come, we might be able to lean on each other for support. Two heads better than one, that kind of thing.'

It was difficult to say more than that without going into a

whole lot of explanation. Basically, Natusch wanted to contact Howie because he felt that there was still a chance that the Colonel, or rather, the men who were backing him, might have some new scheme in hand, despite the presence of the Germans, that could be as significant as the ill-fated Mission Plan. If that were so, he wanted to be in on it – this time, God willing, on something that wasn't jinxed and wouldn't go wrong. But there was another, a more down-to-earth reason for finding Colonel Howie. Natusch had told Evelyn that he and Howie might yet be glad to lean on each other for support, which was true. He knew of a Partisan in Szigetvar who had promised to act as escort through Yugoslavia to Tito's men. If all else should fail, they could find this contact, take him at his word, and join the guerrillas. Natusch also knew two men in Barc, both helpful types, although quite how helpful he couldn't be sure until he'd had some discussion with them: but he couldn't approach any of these people, at least not in safety, until he had a proper Hungarian passport. This was Howie's cue. The Colonel knew no one either in Szigetvar or in Barc. Natusch was almost certain of that, but passports were Howie's line of business, and no doubt he had other aids and artifices up his sleeve.

It was obvious that there would be much to gain from a pooling of resources. If they were to do that, Natusch could cease haring around the countryside with Gestapo thugs in pursuit and begin living at something like normal tempo. Howie's benefit was comparable. He would be able to go to bed at night with a quiet mind, aware that if the need arose, he could travel in comfort to Szigetvar, cross the Drava River in daylight, and be escorted all the way to Partisan H.Q.

Natusch and Barrett stayed in Evelyn Gore-Symes's flat until the afternoon, when Franz Brackel arrived. They rested, moved quickly into her bedroom whenever the doorbell rang, and kept quiet until Evelyn's visitors had left. The Gestapo, as they all knew, were being well served by informers. After lunch, which fulfilled the promise Natusch had made to Barrett the night before, their hostess left them and was away over an hour. She came back, out of breath with excitement and with the effort of climbing six flights of stairs. 'I've seen Franz Brackel,' she announced. Her face was beaming. 'He'll be here in about an hour's time. He's taking you to his friends.'

The blank looks that greeted her brought Evelyn down to earth. 'I forgot,' she said apologetically. 'Of course, you don't know Franz. I should have told you about him. He's a Dutch Army officer, one of about twenty who are living here in Budapest. They were moving about quite openly until the Germans came—' she gave a wry smile '—but they're being more careful now. They escaped last year from a prison camp somewhere in Poland.'

Natusch looked up. 'Their senior officer,' he hazarded. 'Is he Eddie van Hootegem?'

Evelyn nodded. 'Yes,' she said blankly. 'How on earth did you know?'

Natusch waved a deprecating hand as she and Barrett looked at him in astonishment. 'It's no mystery,' he assured them. 'Colonel Howie told me about these chaps a few months back. I remember him saying they were a good crowd. D'you agree with him?'

Evelyn gave another nod, a more emphatic one. 'Yes, a very good crowd.' She spoke simply. 'You'll like them. Franz especially.'

Her prophecy was accurate. At three o'clock, a knock sounded at the outer door and Evelyn returned with a tall red-haired man whom she introduced as Lieutenant Franz Brackel of the Royal Netherlands Army. Natusch liked him on sight. Frank, as he preferred to be called, was a cheerful chap, and that was enough to go on with. Later on, when events began crowding in on them somewhat, he got to like him more. As well as being cheerful, this amiable Dutch officer was to prove himself an uncommonly good man in a tight corner.

Natusch and Barrett said goodbye to Evelyn, and thanked her for all the help she'd given them. 'It's good of you,' Natusch told her. 'You're an angel, Evelyn. Grade One.' As a compliment it sounded flippant but its sincerity wasn't in doubt.

They met Eddie van Hootegem and several of his Dutch officers in a tavern nearby. It was a noisy place, but the Dutchmen had a table in a secluded corner, and after some brisk introductions and a round of brandies, there was a general comparing of notes. Van Hootegem, who spoke well-nigh perfect English, promptly gave Natusch two news items that made him glad he'd met this new ally. He knew where Howie was, and also that the Colonel wanted to leave Hungary. A feeling of disappointment ran through Natusch, but it soon turned to one of relief. They wouldn't be having a last go at the Germans after all, it seemed, which meant that his own stay in Hungary had achieved very little, but Howie's decision to quit the odds-against struggle with the Gestapo was almost a guarantee of continued freedom. With false passports and the Partisan contact, they were as good as home. Natusch turned to van Hootegem. 'We're leaving, too,' he said casually. 'There's a chap at Szigetvar, who says he'll take us through to the Partisans.'

It was the Dutchman's turn to show surprise. 'This man,' he said quickly. 'He is Hungarian? And reliable?'

It occurred to Natusch that both sides might yet profit from this meeting. 'I'm not sure of his nationality,' he said carefully. 'I've not met him myself, but from all I've heard of him, he seems reliable enough.' He smiled faintly. 'So far as anyone's reliable these days, that is. He volunteered to act as escort, if that's anything to go by.'

Van Hootegem's interest mounted. 'Will he take anyone with him,' he persisted, 'or is this a private party?'

Natusch didn't waste words. 'If you chaps want to come with us,' he said bluntly, 'you're welcome. I don't think our contact'll raise any objection. In fact, I'm pretty certain he won't. His original offer was for thirty men, and at present there's only Reg and me. The others were captured. But I'd like to see Colonel Howie before we fix anything. Maybe he'd like to come as well.'

There was a pause as van Hootegem interpreted to those of his friends who didn't speak English. That done, he turned back and offered a large hand. 'Right,' he said cheerfully. 'We go together. All of us. You fix the date as soon as you can. We'll be ready.' The organizer in him took over. 'I'll tell Colonel Howie you want to see him,' he promised. 'And as regards yourselves, perhaps we'd better look after you. Now we know you, we wouldn't want to lose you.' A smile eased the concentration from his face. 'Have you ever slept in a nunnery?' he asked innocently.

The nunnery was a permissible flight of fancy. That night,

Natusch and Barrett went to a Catholic school, dined with the priest, saw none of the nuns, and slept on spring beds. They stayed there two days, and on the third evening Frank Brackel called to say that a meeting with Howie had been arranged. 'But not at his house,' he stressed. 'We will meet him at a rendezvous in a street in Szugliget. The Colonel is—' he searched for the right word '—apprehensive. Of the Germans. You understand?' Natusch understood. Colonel Howie had by no means a monopoly of Gestapo apprehension.

It was dark by the time they reached the residential suburb of Szugliget. Frank Brackel and Natusch walked slowly along a tree-shadowed road, turned and strolled back again, both of them scanning passers-by with feigned disinterest, and with a suspicion already creeping into Natusch's mind that Howie didn't intend to keep the appointment. But he did keep it, and there was a professional touch to his manner of doing so. Natusch didn't see him at all until he materialized at his side, collar up and hat brim pulled right down. He wasn't even sure it was Howie until he heard the familiar voice greeting him.

'Hello, Natusch,' the Colonel began. 'Glad to see you.' He didn't waste words. 'I believe you got no warning of the invasion. I'm sorry about that. My contacts knew about it three days in advance, but they didn't tell me until the day before the Jerries marched in. I couldn't get through to you then. Phones were jammed. Still, you're free now, and I'm glad of it. Good show!'

It occurred to Natusch, forcibly, that the Colonel's tone was unnecessarily breezy and lighthearted. If he had made a little more effort earlier on – had kept his word, in fact – it would have been easier to preserve the freedom that Howie dismissed so lightly. 'What happened to the courier?' he asked. He spoke sharply. 'You were going to send one to warn me if there was any danger. Remember? I was relying on that promise.'

Howie nodded. 'I know,' he said. 'And the promise was kept, too. The courier left here as soon as I knew that the invasion was on. It was the first thing I did.' A hard note crept into his voice. 'He would have reached Szigetvar well ahead of the Gestapo if he hadn't developed cold feet *en route* and gone to Rumania instead. I didn't know he'd failed me until about three days afterwards. It was too late to do anything then. But I *am* glad you got away.'

That remark closed the affair. The only part that had worried Natusch was the uncertainty he'd felt over Colonel Howie's good faith, and that only because he'd trusted him implicitly. He would have staked his liberty, and indeed, had done so, that Howie would act honourably, and he was more than relieved to find his faith justified.

They walked along slowly as Natusch told the Colonel what had happened at Szigetvar, and how the Gestapo had been hot on his heels since then. 'I don't think they'll catch up now,' he went on. 'I'm a few lengths in front. But there'd be less chance still if I could ditch Captain Natusch and start being someone else. Preferably someone they've never heard of.'

Natusch stopped speaking as two men passed them, and wondered fleetingly if everyone who frequented this particular road wore his collar turned up and his hat jammed down hard on his ears. 'I've got another chap with me now,' he resumed. 'An Air Force type. He's on the run, too. Can you fix a couple of passports for us?'

Howie nodded. 'Yes, I'll do that,' he said easily. 'It'll take me two days, perhaps three. I'll give them to Szent-Ivanyi as soon as they're ready, and he'll attend to the stamps and photos. You'll keep the same nationality, of course?' It was more a statement than a question. 'Well, that's easy enough,' the Colonel observed. 'Did you want to see me about anything else?' His nonchalance was infectious.

'I didn't,' Natusch said. 'I've got an escape route to Yugoslavia that might interest you. I hear you're leaving Hungary. Is that right?'

The answer came firmly and emphatically, and it surprised Natusch. 'No, it's wrong,' Howie said. 'Quite wrong. Things don't look so good at the moment, I agree, but I'm not pulling out yet. There's still work to be done here, and I'm staying to do it.' He stopped under a street lamp and answered the unasked question. 'But you're not staying. There's no point in taking a risk like that. The Gestapo know you. If they catch you, and make you talk—' his hands opened expressively '—there'll be a number of people in bad trouble right away. No, Natusch, you go to Yugoslavia, and I'll stay here: but I'll keep that escape route of yours in mind. You can contact me by radio when you reach the Partisans. I may need your help if things get sticky.'

Natusch nodded. 'O.K.,' he agreed. 'It's as you say. I'll leave as soon as you get me those passports.' He indicated Frank Brackel, who so far hadn't done more than exchange a greeting. 'He's coming, too, and about twenty other Dutch officers. Tell me, is the transmitter working?'

Howie smiled. 'Not now,' he said. 'It's in bits, in four or five different places. Transmitters aren't healthy things to have these days. The operator's lying low, too, but we'll be back in business about two weeks from today.'

With that, he and Natusch got down to technicalities. Howie gave his signal code and transmitting dates and times, and Natusch supplied the Szigetvar address, in case Howie had to use it fast. They finished the memory-filing – details like these weren't put to paper – said goodbye there and then, shook hands and parted. That was the last Natusch ever saw of Colonel Charles T. Howie. He learnt later that he stayed in Hungary, as he'd said he would, somehow eluded the Huns, and emerged as chief British Liaison Officer when the Russians entered the country. All told, Colonel Howie did a man-sized job.

He kept his word about the passports. A few days later, Natusch got a message from the Rev. Szent-Ivanyi to call at a neutral Legation that was still open. A Legation, as they both knew, was a safer rendezvous than a private house. Natusch kept the appointment, was received by Szent-Ivanyi and by an official who was polite and helpful, and was given two passports which certified that Barrett and he were now Branko Kovacs and Ladislas Szanto respectively. The generous cleric presented Natusch with a suit which he needed very badly indeed, and also made him a gift of some more money. The New Zealander was doing his best to say an effective thank-you when another Legation official came into the room. 'Excuse me,' he said. 'There's someone outside who claims that he knows you. He saw you . . .'

He got no chance to finish the sentence. A man appeared at the door, pushed the official aside unceremoniously, and dashed into the room. 'Sir!' he called. His voice was high-pitched with excitement. 'Sir! It's me! Sanders! From Szigetvar!' He sat down abruptly, sudden tears of relief welling in his eyes. Tom Sanders, the Hungarian Jew who had brought Howie through from Germany, had turned up again.

Natusch was delighted to see him. Sanders was a reliable man, and his arrival in Budapest meant that four of them had evaded the German trap at Szigetvar, and not three, as he had thought; but he had another, more important reason for welcoming this likeable, ill-used wandering Jew. He wouldn't have to go back to Szigetvar now to make the escape arrangements. Tom Sanders, deputizing for him, would do the job infinitely better. He was a natural-born Hungarian, and what was more, knew who to look for. He and Henry Lowenstein had worked up this contact between them. He slapped Sanders on the back, pumped his hand once again and introduced him to the others. 'Am I glad to see you!' he beamed. 'Where the devil have you been?'

The story that came out was brief and, to a degree, poignant. Sanders's escape had been simple and devoid of frills or danger, which meant, of course, that it was first class. He found a cupboard below the bar counter at Szigetvar, eased his body into a space hardly big enough for a dog, and stayed there until everyone had gone. After that, he walked all the way to Budapest, living on his wits and on the charity of the peasants, and on arrival in the capital, set out to find Howie, whom he knew was there, or failing Howie, Natusch. Intuition had told him that the latter would arrive there some time, and luck led him to select this particular Legation.

The irony of it was that Sanders, a genuine Hungarian, had been unable to get any real help from his own countrymen. He called at the Legation day after day, and kept calling, but no one would accept him at his face value, and he had no papers to dispel the suspicion that he might be a German spy. As a result he had to live rough, and he was hungry more often than not. By contrast, Natusch was now almost sleek with good living, had half a dozen people ready to bed and board him, and influential contacts at ministerial level, and a passport to allay all doubt about his ancestry. If it were to be tested, he'd be in an untenable position, but that was a contingency he didn't fear much. The whole idea of a passport is to certify that its holder is above reproach.

Tom Sanders's arrival couldn't have been better timed. In a day or two, Natusch reflected, the Hungarian would be on his way to Szigetvar to locate the Partisan whom he alone knew by sight, and Reg Barrett, who would very likely travel with him, and who could speak Hungarian reasonably well, would be relieved of having the New Zealander hanging like a millstone round his neck.

Eddie van Hootegem and Frank Brackel approved the change of plan. 'Much safer,' Eddie commented. They were sitting in the tavern that did duty as the Dutch officers' H.Q. 'Very much safer. But what about passports?'

Natusch turned to Barrett and Sanders. He'd had that point in mind himself. 'Here you are,' he said. He handed over the little folders which the Rev. Szent-Ivanyi had just given him. 'Here's your new identities. You're Branko Kovacs and Ladislas Szento now, and if I were you, I wouldn't forget it. I'd learn the details, too. The photos are O.K. They'd pass for any of us. Lowenstein's pal,' he went on, 'the Partisan chap, should be home by now – that's if he ever left home – but if he's not, you'll have to wait for him. I'd stay in Siklos, if I were you. It's only thirty miles away, and it'll be much safer there. If you don't locate the Partisan first go, you can travel in by rail whenever you like, and then go straight back to Siklos.' He grinned at Barrett. 'Try staying at a hotel,' he advised. 'It'll be a damn sight warmer than a church crypt.'

Barrett accepted the passports, examined them, and handed one to Tom Sanders. 'O.K.,' he agreed. 'We'll wait for this fellow if we have to, but not more than a week. If he's not home by then, there'll be no point in hanging on for him any longer. I'd rather come back to Budapest and try again later.' He looked up. 'If we're not back in seven days – say ten at the outside – you'd better start making new arrangements. It'll mean that we've come adrift somewhere. Things do go wrong, you know.'

It was a pessimistic thought that Barrett himself put to flight with the cheeriest of grins, but a couple of days later it came back to Natusch for no particular reason at all, and nothing he could do would budge it. It nagged away at the back of his mind continuously until all doubt was finally and tragically settled.

Next morning, he left the Catholic school, with its priests and non-existent nuns, and went to stay at a Hungarian professor's home. The Rev. Szent-Ivanyi, still actively engaged in intrigue, despite Gestapo suspicion, arranged the move for him. Barrett and Sanders left a Dutch civilian's house – another Szent-Ivanyi arrangement – and caught the early train for Szigetvar. They took with them the hopes of over twenty men, and they left confident and in high spirits. Nothing, any of them felt, could go wrong with this trip. It was foolproof, Gestapo-proof, the easiest venture that any of them had yet undertaken. The two emissaries had money, passport, no language difficulties, and weren't intending to break any German or police regulation. They just couldn't go wrong. In two or three days, perhaps even sooner, they'd be back in Budapest with the Yugoslav route open, and Partisans on the other side of the Drava River waiting for twenty-three Dutch officers and three Englishmen. It would be then that the real planning would start.

Natusch waited in the professor's house. He and his wife were good-natured and hospitable, but Natusch was on edge, and as the days went by and the end of the week loomed up, he had to remind himself that he was a guest and must restrain his impatience. He saw Eddie van Hootegem and Frank Brackel twice, and they too grew increasingly irritable and morose as time went by with still no word from their two colleagues.

They abandoned hope at the end of a fortnight. By then, it was all too clear that somewhere along the route, possibly in Szigetvar itself, disaster had struck, and the well-laid, almost disaster-proof plan had come to naught. They never learnt what had happened to Reg Barrett or Tom Sanders. Not even the post-war years gave any clue. They just vanished.

CHAPTER TEN

THE DOUBLE DUTCHMAN

It was a grievous blow, but it was wartime and they couldn't stop to grieve. Nor, obviously, could anyone be sent to Szigetvar to probe the mystery. There was no one left who could speak Hungarian. 'You'll have to make new arrangements,' Reg Barrett had said. They were prophetic words, almost his last words, and it struck Natusch, looking back, that he must have had a presentiment that the trip would fail.

They took his advice, and made a new arrangement. On the fifteenth day, Frank Brackel followed up a tip from the Rev. Szent-Ivanyi, and spent an hour closeted with an official of yet another Legation. They didn't lack for friends among the neutrals. Eddie van Hootegem and Natusch were waiting for him on his return.

'How did it go, Frank?' Eddie asked. He spoke in English as usual, for Natusch's benefit.

Frank Brackel's face was wreathed in smiles. 'Fine!' he assured them. 'We now have another contact. This one is a Serb, and he is in touch with Tito's Partisans. He says he'll arrange for us to be escorted to their H.Q., but not via Szigetvar. We don't have to go there. There is one difficulty. It will take a week, perhaps two weeks, to fix the arrangements.'

That, in a nutshell, was Frank Brackel's interview with their new Legation contact. The three of them discussed it at length, but half an hour's conversation added nothing worth mentioning – except one item that was to prove more vital to Natusch than any other single happening of the last twelve months.

It came at the end, just as they were about to leave the tavern. Van Hootegem delved in his pocket, brought out an envelope and dropped it into the New Zealander's lap. 'For you,' he said. 'I nearly forgot. It's a present for you. With the compliments of the Royal Dutch Army.'

Natusch picked up the envelope, opened it, and found himself examining van Hootegem's own passport. At least, the details were his. The photograph, heavily impressed by the official stamps, was a blurred likeness that made precise recognition impossible. 'But this is yours,' he protested. 'You can't give it to me. You'll need . . .'

'Take it,' the Dutchman said brusquely. 'It's a copy. My colleague, Lieutenant Bentinck, has made it for you.' He waved away further protest. 'If you are arrested, you can now say that you are Lieutenant Edouard van Hootegem. This passport is duplicated in the police files, and it won't be questioned. It is to be hoped—' he added '—that we are not both of us arrested at the same time.'

Natusch didn't argue further. He needed a passport desperately, and the one that Szent-Ivanyi had obtained for him had gone with Reg Barrett and Tom Sanders on their ill-fated mission. He examined the new document closely, looking for the tell-tale marks that nearly always betray the amateur forger; but it was beyond reproach. Lieutenant Bentinck, as Eddie van Hootegem had said, and had understated, was a competent penman.

The days moved slowly, too slowly for their liking, as they waited for their new-found ally to raise steam. March 1944 ended, and with April the *tempo* of the war increased. They continued to lie low in Budapest, and it galled Natusch to have to do that whilst so much was going on in the world outside.

Around this time, the Russians were providing the bulk of the news. Their three top generals, Zhukov, Koniev and Malinovsky, were making spectacular advances all along the fighting line, with Zhukov's 1st Ukrainian Front, now in the foothills of the Carpathians, setting the pace. The Russian troops were aiming at Hungary through the Tolgyes Pass and the Tartar Pass, and were little more than two hundred miles from Budapest itself. Farther east, the Germans were in worse trouble. The whole of the Crimea seemed on the verge of recapture, and von Kleist's Army Group stood in dire peril. The Russians, so far as Natusch could see, were heading for victory.

The news from the west and the Far East was less spectacular. The Eighth Army, advancing beyond the ruins of Cassino, had invested Rome, but the fury which had smashed Cassino to a heap of rubble had subsided: nor were the 14th Army's skirmishes in Burma anything like a flat-out effort. The Allies, as everyone knew, were brewing up for the Second Front; and once again, it irked the New Zealander that he was missing all these events and sharing none of their excitement.

He left the professor's house at the beginning of April and moved over the river to Buda to the home of two well-to-do Dutch ladies. He made the transfer through the good offices of friends of Eddie van Hootegem and Frank Brackel, because the Gestapo were beginning a new drive against 'undesirables'; but it was precaution rather than panic which inspired the move.

Only definite house searches held any real menace. Natusch went about as he had been doing, and in the city had no fear of being arrested. He was well dressed, had sufficient money and carried van Hootegem's passport to convince any questioner of his identity: but even with documents and money and good friends, life was an uncertain business in Budapest in April 1944. The Germans could smell defeat in the offing, and as was to be expected, the Gestapo had the keenest noses. Their reaction, especially when the long-delayed air raids began, was to fall back on terrorism – all too often on atrocity – as a safeguard against possible Hungarian revolt.

Natusch learnt his lesson almost at first hand. A squad of black-shirted toughs called one evening at a house a few doors from where he was staying, lined up five Polish officers in the dining-room of their flat, riddled them with sub-machine-gun bullets, and then left. Natusch left, too, a few days later, but the five dead Poles stayed where they were, sprawled on a blood-soaked carpet. Everyone in the vicinity knew what had happened, but no one dared enter the flat lest Gestapo spies were watching and waiting to pounce.

A day or so afterwards, there was more bad news. Two Hungarian ministers who had been involved in the Mission Plan fell foul of the Gestapo and were whisked away to the interrogation centre at Schwabb Hegg. From there they went very quickly to the main Gestapo prison in Buda. It was a reminder, and a grim one, because the two ministers weren't seen again, that the Geheime Staatspolizei still intended to round up everyone who had had anything to do with the Mission.

Natusch didn't understand then why they were attaching such importance to a plot which had failed so completely, but Colonel Howie and his friends had been fishing in deeper waters than any of them realized. A much bigger scheme lay behind the Mission Plan. They knew nothing of it. The Germans learnt little, but what they did get was very clearly dynamite, although it didn't include any names that really mattered; nor could the Abwehr, for all its efforts, discover who was the instigator of this larger plot. He, the instigator, had many men shielding him and keeping his affairs secret. He wasn't a captain, or a major, or even a general. He was Franklin D. Roosevelt, President of the United States of America.

Roosevelt produced his idea at the Big Three meeting at Teheran in November 1943. He had an eye to the future, and as befitted the leader of a nation, a capacity to think big. He outlined his proposal. Let the Allies land on the Istrian peninsula at the head of the Adriatic, he suggested, let them capture Trieste and Fiume, and drive on through the Ljubljana Gap to Vienna. That way – if the planning was done well and executed boldly – the war would be over in a matter of months.

Winston Churchill agreed with his American colleague unreservedly. It was an idea after his own heart. Probably it was at this stage that someone thought of an obvious refinement to the plan, of detaching Hungary from her German ally, and certainly the idea prospered as the weeks went by and it became clear that Hungary was willing to be detached. The Mission was a natural consequence of this line of thought; but Hitler's generals could have saved their worrying for the leaner times that lay ahead. Stalin, third man of the Teheran trio, after cogitating for far too long, gave a delayed but wholly uncompromisng No to Roosevelt's suggestion. He was adamant in his refusal to endorse the plan or even to consider it. What *he* wanted, he said brusquely, was a landing in France. What was more, he wanted it fast.

Roosevelt, performing a volte-face that was as inexplicable as it was surprising, swung over to Stalin's idea, which left Churchill in a minority of one. Winston was infuriated, was incensed almost but not quite beyond words, but in the end he had to change his mind too, and the Mission, now fully planned and in the operational stage, died at that precise moment.

Stalin's inflexibility was based, as later events proved, on a very cogent reason. His persistence cost Hungary her freedom, and at a much lower level, cost Colonel Howie and his associates, both British and Hungarian, the success of a long-cherished scheme; but although the Mission Project had been stillborn, the fears it had occasioned didn't subside. The Germans were determined to root out all those who had had anything to do with the intrigue and to destroy them utterly. Such men, they considered – and rightly so – were dangerous.

Frank Brackel's Legation contact didn't keep them waiting long. During the second week of April 1944 he sent word through that the escape route was now open, and asked them to confirm the number of would-be travellers who wanted to use it. Brackel and Natusch rushed off jubilantly to the tavern, gave them the news, and promptly got a shock that almost knocked the fight out of them.

'We're not going,' the officers' spokesman repeated. For once, Eddie van Hootegem was not with them. 'We've changed our minds. Willem and Piet have seen Colonel Howie, and he says that the Russians will be here in Budapest inside three months. We believe him, so there's no point in risking our necks going to Yugoslavia. We're doing all right here. All we have to do is sit tight and let the Russkies kick the Bosch out of Hungary.' The Dutchman shrugged his shoulders. 'Why take chances?'

Neither Brackel nor Natusch could make him change his opinion, nor could they influence any of his friends. They were in full song when Eddie van Hootegem strolled into the tavern and threw his weight into the argument, but even that did no good. Colonel Howie, the defecting officers repeated, was at the fountain-head and knew better than they did what was going on. If Howie said Russkies in three months, three months it was, and it ill behoved anyone to contradict him.

Van Hootegem had to give in, of course, and the result was precisely what he feared. The Legation contact, whose minimum stake in this game was his own life, decided that he wasn't going to risk it for a bunch of fainthearts who couldn't make up their minds whether they wanted to be helped or not. Natusch didn't blame him.

At this point, the New Zealander seemed to have come up against a brick wall. Neither he nor van Hootegem nor Frank Brackel had any more contacts, nor any escape route other than the too-hazardous one through Szigetvar, and Gestapo agents were beginning to unravel the tangle of their affairs. They were still remote, but the writing was on the wall and Natusch began taking greater care. He was now back in Buda, at the home of the two Dutch ladies, and he didn't go out unnecessarily. When he did, he had his passport handy, kept an eye open for anyone trailing him, and didn't board or leave tramcars unless they were moving. But this kind of existence, which was being widely adopted, wasn't a happy one, nor very safe, nor was it getting him anywhere. But for Frank Brackel's injunction, he would have left Budapest, on his own if necessary, and made tracks for Barc.

Frank was insistent. 'Don't go,' he urged. 'Not yet. I think I am having success.' He dug deep into his store of English colloquialisms and brought out a winner. 'The kettle is on the boil,' he announced.

He wouldn't commit himself beyond that, but there was a confidence about him that made Natusch think twice about his own plan. 'Your kettle had better boil fast,' he growled. 'I'm damned if I can see any steam from it.'

But Frank wasn't joking. A few days later he came back, his cheery face wreathed in its biggest-ever grin. 'He has changed his mind,' he announced. 'The chap at the Legation. The one who said No. He is taking us to Yugoslavia in four days' time. It is good, yes?'

The all-clear from the contact came through on 26th April. This time it concerned ten of them, van Hootegem, Brackel, Natusch and seven of the Dutch officers, and with it came a suggestion that they should all take extra care; but the Legation official's prudence seemed unnecessary. Just for a change, life in Budapest reverted almost to normal, Gestapo activity eased off, and the war itself entered a momentary lull. On Friday, 28th April, Natusch got up feeling bright and cheerful. It was a fine sunny morning, with new leaves on the trees, flowers blooming in the more sheltered gardens, and two days to go before they moved off.

Towards evening, Frank Brackel called for him, and they set off for their dinner engagement at the house of one of Frank's friends. *En route*, they picked up an Air Force officer named Joob Sengor, one of the seven Dutch officers who had preferred their counsel to Colonel Howie's. Natusch was interested to meet Joob. He had heard Eddie van Hootegem speak highly of him, and had visualized a beefy character with steady eyes and an iron handshake. Joob wasn't a bit like that. He was a dapper man, neat and precise, and only one part of Natusch's estimate was correct. His gaze was level, and it had a quality to it that was instantly reassuring.

Dinner began early, at the friend's house, and in a style that brought back nostalgic memories of special occasions of pre-war days. An atmosphere of cordiality was quickly established, and eight o'clock found the company seated around a polished table, with aperitifs finished, and the first course already on its way from the kitchen.

There were seven of them at table, the host and his wife, the anonymous Legation official and his lady, and the three Allied soldiers. Eddie van Hootegem, pleading a prior engagement, had sent apologies, and Frank Brackel conveyed them with an old-world charm that befitted the surroundings. Dinner was served, and Natusch was enjoying a delicately flavoured *consommé paysanne*, and feeling that life wasn't so bad after all, when faintly, above the murmur of the dinner talk, a doorbell sounded. No one seemed to notice it. Natusch did, because small noises like footsteps and doorbells registered with him, but after a moment's unease, he relaxed. No today, he thought. Today's guaranteed. The maid was on the point of removing his soup dish when it became clear, suddenly and alarmingly clear, that today held no special protection.

The door leading to the kitchen opened abruptly. Three men entered the room, fanned out, and stood facing the assembly, the ones on either side of the door holding their right hands significantly in their pockets. All wore plain clothes and the trench coats that these days were the uniform of secret police pretty well everywhere. The leader of the trio gazed at the silent company at the table. He seemed to be searching for someone. Suddenly he spoke. 'Up!' he ordered.

The command came in German, but with an inflection that made it clear that this man was Hungarian; and possibly the more to be feared for that. They rose, and absent-mindedly Natusch put a hand to his pocket.

The intruders immediately dropped all pretence. Pistols leapt from the pockets of the two lesser men and covered him. Their leader, relieved perhaps at finding someone on whom to concentrate his attention, came over, snarled 'Hande Hoch!' and began firing questions rapidly and once again in German. That got him nowhere, because Natusch told him that he was a Hollander and didn't understand Deutsch, and a second and unexpected line of attack followed. 'Show me your passport!' The policeman, in quick pantomime, opened an imaginary folder and glared at his victim. 'Passport, you oaf!' he barked. Natusch said 'Ah!' as if in relief, and produced his Dutch identity card.

The little folder quietened the Gestapo man. He moved on, checked the others' passports, and betrayed surprise and indecision when he found all were in order. It was now the host's turn to attack. Backed by his Legation friend, he rounded on the intruders. 'What are you doing here?' he demanded. 'Who sent you? Who gave you the authority to . . .?' An upraised hand halted him. 'The men—' the policeman said bleakly and with a finality that overrode objection '—will come with us. The women will stay here.'

Natusch could have dodged away easily enough as they walked through the garden. It was a dark night and the three policemen weren't on the alert, but he didn't go because just then there seemed no point in going, and it would have brought suspicion on his friends. There'd been a mistake and they were being taken for a routine check by the Hungarian police. Once they were satisfied, release would be automatic. Nor was there any reason why the police shouldn't be satisfied. The host and the Legation official were above suspicion, Frank Brackel and Joob Sengor had proper passports made out in their own names, and Roy Natusch was now Eddie van Hootegem, with papers to prove it.

At first, all went well at police headquarters in Pest. They got their papers back, and surprisingly, an apology in German from the leader of the trio who had arrested them. 'I'm sorry we had to bring you here,' he said. He was polite and almost friendly, different altogether from the hard character they'd seen an hour before. 'We got a report through and we had to check it. It was wrong.' He didn't elaborate. 'The two civilian gentlemen may go now. The car is waiting. You others—' he turned to Frank, Joob and Natusch '—will have to stay here tonight, I'm afraid. My chief will see you tomorrow morning.'

There was no budging that decision. The security man smiled at Frank Brackel's tirade, ignored an offer to return next day at any time he liked to mention, and mounted a guard. It was at this point that Natusch felt the first prickling of uneasiness. He was being held, admittedly by an unusually solicitous gaoler, but it didn't alter the fact that he was no longer a free man. He didn't like it.

The morning brought no comfort. Frank, and then Joob, went into the police chief's office, and came out fairly quickly, which encouraged Natusch for his own visit. He went in feeling that for once he'd been wasting valuable worry; but he was soon disillusioned. A Hungarian colonel of gendarmerie surveyed him coldly from behind a huge desk. He was wearing a swastika armband. A portrait of the Fuehrer on the wall behind glanced down equally disapprovingly, and on right- and left-hand sides of the colonel stood Gestapo officers whom he guessed correctly were from Schwabb Hegg.

For a few minutes, Natusch's fate hung in the balance. The three Nazis conferred together, examined his passport, picked up Frank Brackel's and Joob Sengor's and had another look at them, but asked no questions. Natusch stood before them stolidly, ignoring them like a Dutch officer would have done, silently cheering the colonel who was trying to persuade his colleagues that enough time had been wasted already. But the Gestapo were never eager to release prisoners. The one on the right made up his mind, overruled the colonel – which showed where the real power lay and glanced at the New Zealander. 'Kommen sie mit,' he said briefly. 'Die andere zwei auch.'

They went to Schwabb Hegg in a couple of Opel saloon cars. The interrogation centre was a good distance away, through Pest, over the Danube, and then up a long hill, and the journey took sufficient time for Natusch to appreciate the gravity of his position. At Schwabb Hegg, the Nazis would take one look at his passport and either address him in German, in which he wasn't fluent, or call in their Dutch interpreter. He didn't speak a word of Dutch, which left bluff as his only resource. But bluff had been kind to him in the past. It might yet succeed . . .

The two Gestapo officers began their questioning in leisurely fashion. Natusch told them, in indifferent German, that he was Lieutenant Edouard van Hootegem and that he had escaped from a camp near Stanislau in Poland. If he could have understood and answered the questions that followed, perhaps Frank, Joob and he would have been free by lunchtime, but the Gestapo insisted on precise answers and his German wasn't up to it. The senior officer pressed a bell and was saying someting about 'Hollandisch sprecher' when Natusch realized that it was time to begin the bluffing. 'I am a Dutch officer,' he said slowly and distinctly, 'but I do not speak Dutch. Does anyone here understand English?'

If the Fuehrer himself had walked into the room just then, the two Gestapo men could hardly have dropped their bored looks faster. Their eyebrows shot up simultaneously and the lesser of the two let his jaw drop a little, but apart from that, both did credit to their training. Gestapo personnel did not show emotion. The senior officer pressed his bell a second time, amended his request to 'Englischer sprecher', and looked at Natusch with sudden interest.

A moment or two later, a middle-aged Frau bustled into the room. Her English was faultless, but her services weren't really needed. The balloon had gone up now, and Schwabb Hegg was no longer the right setting for this particular interrogation. Schwabb Hegg sorted out a riff-raff of petty defaulters, deserters, and black marketeers, and a Dutch officer, allegedly from Poland, currently resident in Hungary, speaking English but not Dutch, was clearly destined for the main Gestapo prison in Buda and for the well-known and much-feared special interrogation technique that rarely – the Germans said never – failed to detect an impostor. Frank Brackel and Joob Sengor, as associates and possible accomplices, would also go there. The net was closing fast.

There were no Opel saloons this time, but instead a black

Gestapo van that had steel doors and guards who carried machine-pistols. The three men reached the Buda prison intact, were met by an Oberfeldwebel who was expecting them, and were escorted to the top floor of the building. There, they were searched for the third time in one day, but neither the Oberfeldwebel nor his men noticed anything unusual. Natusch didn't intend them to. Since 1941, he'd been searched too often not to profit from experience, and this time, despite having to strip naked, he managed to conceal one hundred American dollars, five hundred *pengös*, his Dutch identity card and his watch, simply by changing the lot rapidly and with a conjuror's dexterity from one hand to the other.

The first battle of wills came as soon as they were once again dressed. The warrant officer pointed a finger. 'Over there,' he ordered curtly. 'Face the wall. Stand to attention. *Move!!*' None of them stirred, and the Gestapo man's expression changed from boredom to astonishment, and more quickly, from astonishment to fury. 'Schnell!!' he roared. 'Schwein!!!'

Natusch looked with interest, first at him and then at Frank Brackel. The German was not alone in his anger. The big Dutchman was now sitting bolt upright, his red hair bristling, his fists white, clenched on the arms of the wooden chair. He rose stiffly, his mouth a thin line, his nostrils distended with a rage that wasn't assumed, and looked down on the Oberfeldwebel. 'We will *not* face your wall like common criminals,' he began. The German 'nicht' came from between Frank's clenched teeth so savagely that for a moment Natusch thought he would hit this Hun. 'Nor will we stand to attention. We are officers of the Royal Dutch Army and we are your superiors in rank. You will remember that, Herr Oberfeldwebel. None of us is required to stand to attention when speaking to you. We follow the same military etiquette as the Wehrmacht. The Wehrmacht' – he added, without relenting any of his ice-cold hostility '—will support us in this.'

The last sentence probably saved them from some particularly ferocious handling. The veins in the German N.C.O.s neck bulged, and his men moved forward ominously, awaiting the word; but Frank Brackel had laid his stress in the right place. The Wehrmacht still carried weight in Reich affairs, and as yet the Gestapo hesitated to ride roughshod over their conventions. That saved them, but by a hair's-breadth. The Oberfeldwebel banged his fist on the table, bawled curses in an endeavour to save face, flung instructions to the waiting gaolers and stormed out of the room.

His prisoners weren't long in following. Half a dozen guards escorted them along corridors patrolled by S.S. men to a cell in what was clearly the less salubrious part of the prison. They weren't separated, but as the steel door clanged shut they realized that they didn't have to thank anyone for this consideration. They were together still because the main prison was full, was overfull, and this cell one of the very few still unoccupied.

Even so, if anyone had cared, they could almost certainly have been given better accommodation. The cell was a dirty dingy hole, about ten feet by six, with two narrow beds to cater for three of them, and the far wall monopolized by a closet that was both faulty and primitive. Their status was also distinctly unhealthy. 'We'll be kept here for a week,' Frank Brackel announced, his anger now dissipated. 'Maybe longer. Don't worry,' he added. 'It's safer to talk here.' He smiled reassurance as Natusch, distressed at being the unwitting cause of the present calamity, offered a futile apology. 'It is not your fault, Roy,' he said. 'These things happen in war, remember. But I am right. We'll not get out of here quickly. The last thing that that Feldwebel pigdog said was "Let them rot," so there's a week for you to begin with.' Joob Sengor nodded. 'It will be more,' he said. 'Much more. The prison is full, remember.'

Frank was less pessimistic. 'But we will not stay for ever,' he observed. He turned to Natusch. 'Nor will they forget us. And I will tell you what will happen now. We are in danger. The Gestapo will contact our old camp at Stanislau in Poland, and they will check our identities there. They will also check at XXI Department in Buda, as a matter of routine, but that won't get them anywhere. Joob and I are genuine, and I think Colonel Utassy will vouch that you're Eddie van Hootegem.' Frank sniffed and pulled a face. 'There are better cells than this,' he said firmly. 'But never mind. What is more important, Roy, is that you do not speak Dutch. Until you can explain, precisely, why you don't know your own language, I think we will all remain in this cell. Or go to a worse one.' He looked grim. 'You have a special interrogation ahead of you, and you must pass it. It will be bad if you don't. For all of us. In future, we will call you Eddie. All the time. And now let us think. We have to convince these Germans that you *are* Eddie.'

They thought hard. Very hard, because they were now in great danger, as Frank Brackel had stressed. The coming interrogation was vital, could easily be a matter of life or death, and they had only their own wits to support them. They would need them, too, because there was far more to the proposed deception than merely explaining how it was that Natusch, a Dutchman, couldn't speak Dutch. They tackled that item last, and began their scheming immediately. There was no time to lose and no question about the need for meticulous briefing. Gestapo interrogators were, by nature and by training, sceptical men. They were also thorough, and would hardly confine their questions to language difficulties. Frank and Joob agreed that the German P.O.W. files would be unlikely to reveal much about van Hootegem, but as Natusch now *was* van Hootegem, the minimum that he had to know about him, in short, was everything. He had to learn more than that. 'More' was a tall order that anticipated the questioning to come, and involved memorizing not only family and personal details, but also such things as the Battle of Holland – in minute detail – the geography of Amsterdam and other places which he'd never visited, his journey as the captive van Hootegem from Holland to Nuremburg Langwasser, and from there to Stanislau in Poland. He had to be able to describe personalities in these two camps and to draw detailed plans of either.

At this point, an hour or so later, and with his pupil's newly gained knowledge still very sketchy, Frank Brackel, who had been with Eddie van Hootegem all along and who knew everything there was to know about him, handed over to Joob Sengor, who continued Natusch's coaching with a review of recent Dutch history. When he had finished that, he mentioned details of the Royal Family, the names of prominent people, and in short, all the topical items that even an exiled Dutchman would be expected to know.

The long and intensive tuition spread itself over a whole week, with constant repetition and checking and cross-checking, and somehow Natusch managed to remember almost everything. Looking back, it seems a fantastic feat of memory, but given the spur, a man can reach beyond his normal limit. The New Zealander had plenty of incentive; almost too much. He realized precisely what was at stake, and knew the penalty of failure; and by dint of concentrated effort during the day, and sometimes the night, he filed away every scrap of information that Frank and Joob could give him. At the end of the week his face had become drawn and slightly haggard with the terrific mental stress, but all three men now felt fairly confident that no one who didn't know the real van Hootegem personally would spot the deception.

The language difficulty, which at first sight had seemed almost insuperable, didn't hold them up for long. They had to explain a Dutch national who spoke English instead of Dutch, so they did the obvious thing, and reaching back over the years, exiled the infant van Hootegem from Holland to the Dutch East Indies before he could speak at all. That was plausible and it allowed them scope. From the Indies they sent him to an English preparatory school in Singapore, and from there, to New Zealand for his secondary schooling and adolescence. That move explained both the English language and the New Zealand accent, and all that now remained was to enlist the fictitious van Hootegem in the Dutch Army.

This part wasn't easy at all. They pondered over various methods, faulted them all, and were on the verge of despair when Joob Sengor found the perfect answer. His inspiration dated back to 1939, when Britain was supplying Holland with small arms, including Vickers and Lewis machine-guns. These weapons, as Joob pointed out, aren't as simple as experts make out, and naturally the Dutch authorities wanted all the instructors they could get. It seemed the ideal way to bring Eddie van Hootegem back to his mother country. He had never relinquished his Dutch nationality, and his skill with the heavy Vickers outweighed the fact that he couldn't talk about it in Dutch. Even with that handicap he was welcome, because at the time Holland really was desperate for instructors, and van Hootegem held the highest qualifications. To supply them, they changed his secondary education from New Zealand to Australia, and graduated him from the Duntroon Military College as a small-arms specialist.

That background, they felt, should convince even the most sceptical interrogator that van Hootegem had nothing to hide. A knowledge test on guns certainly wouldn't trip him. Natusch had trained with the Lewis and Bren and had used a Vickers in Greece at a time when the men knew their weapons were the ones who survived. He would, he felt, be happy to face the Gestapo on that score. As far as machine-guns were concerned, he was confident that anything the Huns could do, he could do better.

CHAPTER ELEVEN

HOLE IN THE WEB

THEY had to wait another three days before the van Hootegem story was tested. The delay saw them into their second week in Buda prison, and it wasn't a happy time. The cell they were in was small, had only two beds, and they weren't allowed exercise. Added to that, the Gestapo rations were revolting, even by prison standards, and their uncleaned cell had a noisome stench. One got used to it after a while, but it gripped newcomers by the throat and shook them.

There were also bugs. In these places there are always bugs, and even with practice it is difficult to ignore them. It is a moot point which is worse – the cloying odour of the crushed insect or the bite of the brute. They tend to be vicious even in death. On the morning when the interrogation N.C.O. appeared, he came close to being welcomed, but it seemed that he, too, had a sting in his tail. He clicked his heels, Heil-Hitlered, and barked 'Lieutenant Brackel, Lieutenant Sengor, come!' He didn't enlarge on the order, and the steel door banged in Natusch's face before the full impact of it struck him.

The New Zealander's fears, so far kept under restraint, reasserted themselves instantly. Frank and Joob had gone. He was alone. That could mean that the Gestapo knew his real identity – had known it all along – and were toying with him like a cat with a mouse. He tried to suppress the thought, but it wouldn't be suppressed. It stayed with him in that hot, bug-ridden cell all morning and most of the afternoon, turning slowly from suspicion to certainty as the day dragged on.

He had almost given up hope when the door suddenly opened, and Frank and Joob marched back into the cell, an escort hard on their heels. Frank gave a warning look and played hard to his gallery. 'Hello, Eddie,' was his greeting. 'Looks like we'll be released in a day or two now. Good news, eh?' He dropped his voice as the guard left. 'I don't know why they didn't take you,' he said, 'but I don't think it means anything. They are very busy – how do you say it? – mad busy, yes? We have been waiting all day. They'll probably send for you tomorrow.'

Frank Brackel was a good prophet. Next morning, the interrogation N.C.O. called again, and soon afterwards Natusch found himself sitting in a room on the ground floor, with a dozen other people, waiting. By now, he had conquered his earlier fears. Several Jews were there too, also waiting, but they stood at the back of the room. In German prisons, Jews did not sit.

The interrogation office was a pleasant place. It was as wholesome as the cell was distasteful, and had two large windows overlooking a garden in which the promise of spring was being amply fulfilled. It was well furnished, with discreet leather upholstery and carved woodwork emphasizing its masculinity and harmonizing with the watercolours and sporting prints on the walls. But there was a cuckoo in the nest. The inevitable oversized portrait of Hitler, this time with the right hand held palm outwards at shoulder level, as if pronouncing a blessing, starved the prints and watercolours of the attention they merited. It was a garish portrait, a vulgar thing that dominated the room and hung directly above the two men who were watching the newcomer silently and with clinical interest from behind a steel desk. One of the men, the elder of the two, was in plain clothes. His colleague was a young S.S. Hauptmann, who gazed at Natusch through rimless glasses.

The plain-clothes man did most of the questioning. He went on for a while before speaking briefly to his uniformed subordinate, who handed him a letter which Natusch, suddenly remembering Frank Brackel's prophecy, guessed correctly was written by Colonel Lorand Utassy of the Hungarian XXI Department. He knew what would be in that letter, and the confidence that had begun slowly to seep away returned fast. The Colonel, at the moment when it mattered most, had come to his aid, had vouched for him. It was more than likely, therefore, that he wouldn't be under real suspicion after all. His morale soared. Utassy, of necessity in close liaison with the Germans, and trusted by them, had saved him.

And so it proved. The two Germans accepted, without much ado, that he was Lieutenant Edouard van Hootegem of the Royal Dutch Army, and Natusch passed a silent vote of thanks to the Colonel as they moved on to the next hurdle. Here, he gave the plain-clothes man all his attention. He needed to. The Germans didn't doubt that he was a genuine Dutchman. Colonel Utassy's assurance had settled that point satisfactorily, but the language problem was too intriguing to be passed over lightly. 'And you don't speak Dutch?' the older man repeated incredulously. He stroked his chin, tried to fathom the mystery himself, and gave up. 'Why?'

Natusch told him why. He spoke easily, avoided being glib with detail, and was stopped several times and asked to supply it. He'd been taken to Java, he said, when he was a few months old, and had gone from there to Singapore. The plain-clothes man held up his hand. 'What town in Java?' he inquired. His English, Natusch noticed, was stilted and less accurate than his colleague's. 'Batavia,' he answered. 'The capital.' The Hauptmann, following the lead he had been given, opened an atlas, found the map he wanted, and looked up again. 'And how far is it from Batavia to Singapore?' he challenged.

Natusch hid his relief. If the usual keen and incisive Gestapo questioning was being thrown overboard for trivialities like this, he might well have an easy passage. He didn't hesitate. Joob Sengor had taken him over the geography and customs of the East Indies thoroughly, and he knew everything that could reasonably be expected of him. 'It's about three hundred miles,' he replied. 'But I can't tell you much about the journey. I was only four years old at the time.'

The Hauptmann conceded the point, and Natusch went on explaining why he didn't speak Dutch. He did the job convincingly. They went from Singapore to Auckland, from there to Duntroon in Australia, and from Duntroon to Amsterdam. A good many questions were fired *en route*, some of them ticklish ones, but none that he couldn't answer. Nor did the unexpectedly amiable tone of the interrogation deceive him. The Gestapo didn't always show their brutal side.

In the main they were intelligent men, and they could easily swing from one extreme of conduct to another to suit their own purposes, but behind the façade always – it paid to remember it – lay ruthlessness and savagery. They were thorough, too, with a Teuton thoroughness that gave one reason why the Buda prison was so overcrowded with suspects.

Natusch's examination, which he had thought optimistically, and perhaps guilelessly, was finished, had only just begun. The plain-clothes man lit a cigarette, abandoned the East Indies and travel, and with all the time in the world, apparently, commenced a new series of questions on Dutch personalities and political events. He was well informed, and it was here that the hard work, the memory filing and the constant memory checks paid their dividends. Natusch answered almost but not quite all the questions that were put to him, stumbled deliberately once or twice to make sure that he didn't sound rehearsed, and let his confidence grow noticeably as the questioning slowly returned to a more personal level.

Here, he had no hesitation at all. He described how he had fought, during the invasion of Holland, at Vaalhaven Airport, and later, on the Maas River. He drew a map of the Hertogenbosch area that interested the plain-clothes man, pulled up his chair, and began telling him and the S.S. officer how he would have fought the battle himself if he'd been in charge. That move, almost bound to succeed with any serving officer, sidetracked the questioning efficiently. Both the Gestapo official and the young Hauptmann had been in Holland in 1940, and both were full of the superiority of German tactics. Natusch listened to them carefully. He had studied this campaign minutely with Frank Brackel. In the end he agreed, a shade reluctantly, that the new Wehrmacht strategy of Blitzkreig, of parachutists and quick-moving Panzer forces backed by the Luftwaffe's Stuka dive-bombers, had outdated all other contemporary military thinking. They came back gradually to reality, but by this time, Natusch had been offered and had accepted a cigarette, and had made several points of his own on a basis of equality.

He could never have done it if the two Germans had held the slightest doubt about his identity: nor, perhaps, if their boredom with the too-frequent interrogation of suspects who were plainly terrified of them had not made them welcome an interlude such as this.

There wasn't much left now. With all suspicion dispelled, the Germans came almost languidly to the real purpose of the interview. The plain-clothes man glanced at the file in front of him, read a few passages at random, and looked up. 'How long have you been in Hungary?' he asked.

Natusch answered promptly. 'Nearly four months. We escaped from Stanislau in January.'

'Have you met any English officers since you came here?'

'No.'

'Did you know that there were English officers in Hungary?'

Natusch nodded. This was common knowledge. 'Yes,' he said. 'I've heard about them several times, but so far I've not met any.'

The Gestapo man paused for emphasis. 'I want you to think carefully,' he stressed. 'Have you ever heard of a Colonel Howie?'

Natusch thought for a moment and then shook his head slowly. 'No,' he replied. 'I haven't.'

'Or Captain Natusch? From Szigetvar?'

The New Zealander's brow furrowed. 'Captain who?' he asked.

'Captain Natusch,' the German repeated. 'It is an unusual name, but he is English. Have you seen him?' He persisted. 'Or heard of him?'

Natusch shook his head again, this time firmly. 'No,' he said emphatically. 'I've never met these officers. This is the first time I've heard of either of them.'

The German studied his expression closely for a few moments and then grunted. 'That is good,' he said. His voice held a trace of the earlier harshness and despotism. 'Good for you, that is. We want those men. Badly. We will find them, too.'

The questioning finished there. It had been an unusual interview, with no raised voices, no threats, and very little *Herrenvolk* arrogance. Natusch had won through more easily than any of them had thought possible because he'd been too well drilled by Frank Brackel and Joob Sengor to be tripped by the Gestapo questions, and also because Colonel Utassy had testified for him. He realized very clearly that but for the timely support of all three men, blows and loud voices would almost certainly have replaced what by Gestapo standards had been tantamount to a friendly discussion.

Frank Brackel was non-committal about the prospects of an early release. The Hauptmann had intimated that they might be registered as aliens and allowed to work in Budapest, but he had made no promise. 'I will refer the matter to Berlin,' he had said. 'You will have to wait.' They did wait, and Frank's apathy was justified. Twelve days went by, and at the end of them they were still in their stinking cell, still eating the same atrocious food – or most of it – and still enduring the bugs. But the twelfth day, which outside the Buda prison dawned clear and sunny, brought bad news. It seemed that they weren't being allowed to stay in Hungary after all. The Fuehrer, despite being preoccupied with more pressing matters, had found time to issue an order to the effect that recaptured officers of all nationalities were to be sent to Germany and kept there. They would leave, the Hauptmann told them, within the week.

Frank and Joob smiled in relief. To them the news meant a release from this terrible prison, and that feeling was uppermost in their minds. Natusch was less intrigued. He didn't like this Gestapo hell-hole any more than they did, but he'd been accepted here as a non-Dutch-speaking Dutchman, and he didn't think that the same good fortune would attend him at an Oflag. He detached a short iron bar from one of the beds and slid it down the seam of his civilian overcoat. There was a journey ahead, and given better luck than he'd been shown recently, it was just possible that he wouldn't complete it.

The precaution was wasted. Two days later, a contingent of almost a hundred Hungarians, Poles, French, Jews and nondescripts left the Buda prison and assembled under heavy guard outside the railway station. Natusch and his friends were with them, but not of them. Two guards kept them from mingling with the crowd, and stayed with them throughout the long journey. The iron bar proved useless. They travelled in a fast troop train, with doors locked and guards patrolling the corridors, and Natusch was reduced to the timeworn dodge of visiting the lavatory to win himself a little elbow room. That manoeuvre was also profitless. He went when the engine was puffing up an incline and he would have jumped from the train, given a chance, but chance was denied him. There was no window in the toilet.

They were in the train all day. It went from the main line to a rural line, was shunted in and out of sidings twice, and eventually, towards dusk, deposited its weary passengers at a small and anonymous station. A half-hour's march brought them to what was obviously a reception and transit camp.

A big surprise came next morning. The three Dutchmen, still segregated from the others, were being escorted to the wash house when a startled shout made Natusch jump. 'Hey!' someone called. 'Look who's here! It's the Captain!' Standing by the wire was Joe Crolla, one of the Szigetvar men.

The New Zealander went hot and cold in turn. Providentially, Joe Crolla hadn't mentioned the word 'Natusch', and he made urgent signs to him. 'Break it down, Joe,' he pleaded. 'I'm a Dutchman now. Don't forget it. See you later.'

Joe Crolla's brow furrowed, but the mind behind it worked fast. Natusch was standing under the shower, enjoying the cold freshness of the jets, when a thin, worried-looking man came into the wash house, glanced around, and walked towards him. It was his old friend, Henry Lowenstein.

Henry greeted him eagerly. 'Hello, sir,' he said. 'Glad to see you. Joe Crolla told me you were here, but he said something about you pretending to be a Dutchman. I didn't understand him properly.' He made reassuring gestures. 'Don't worry about the guards, sir. They won't interfere. I'm the interpreter here.'

Natusch questioned Henry whilst he was drying himself. He was at Camp 17A, he learnt, in Austria, some fifteen miles from Hegyshalom, a town on the Austro-Hungarian frontier. 17A was a P.O.W. camp for British, French, and Russian soldiers, and also acted as a staging post for other nationalities.

The last remark confirmed Natusch's intuition that he was once again in imminent danger. Frank Brackel had gathered from their train escorts that they were unlikely to remain at 17A, and might be sent on to a Dutch Oflag at Neubrandenberg, some seventy miles north of Berlin. Mention of 'staging post' turned possibility into near-certainty, and

Natusch could visualize in detail what would happen if he were to reach Neubrandenberg. There would be an interpreter there waiting to check the new arrivals, which meant that he would once again have to clear the high hurdle of his inability to speak Dutch, this time without Colonel Lorand Utassy to allay enemy suspicion and probably without either Frank or Joob at hand to vouch for him. The camp authorities would label him an impostor, which would mean reference to the central authorities and thence to the Gestapo. The New Zealander cast around for some other solution to this latest impasse and shrugged his shoulders as he realized that he had but one answer to offer.

He turned to the waiting Lowenstein. The guards were becoming restive. 'I need your help, Henry,' he said quickly. 'We're being sent to Neubrandenberg, and I'm not keen on getting there. I want a set of papers to pass as an I-ty. It's urgent.' He picked up his towel as the guards' impatience increased. 'And thanks, Henry. You're a good sort. If you can, make it three sets.' It seemed unlikely that Frank and Joob, who had already given him escape priority, would get an opportunity to leave with him, but it was as well to be prepared.

He didn't see Lowenstein again that day, but there were signs that the Palestinian wasn't spending it idly. Next morning, McGregor, another stalwart from Szigetvar, brought in the rations, together with word that Henry had been up half the night working on his forgeries, which was encouraging news. One set of papers, it appeared, was almost ready.

McGregor had more to say, but this time it concerned reminiscence rather than current planning. Natusch's escape at Szigetvar, McGregor recounted, had led to a rare hullabaloo. The young Wehrmacht officer, it seemed, had paled when the fusillade of shots sounded outside the *Gasthaus*, had recovered his calm as the distracted Gestapo N.C.O. burst in shouting 'He's gone! He's gone!' and had intervened when a roar of cheering and booing from the assembly saw the infuriated Obergefreiter reaching for his pistol.

The Szigetvar men, Natusch learnt, had been taken south to Belgrade, where Dai Davies and Norman McLean had won free from a locked goods wagon at the height of an air raid. From Belgrade, those who were left had travelled northwards to Camp 17A. There were, McGregor confided, several good escape schemes brewing right now.

Henry Lowenstein appeared a few hours later and got past the guards without difficulty. 'Here you are, sir,' he said. 'It's finished.' He glanced around nervously. 'Best hide it. I'm not sure about these guards.' Natusch put the slim package he'd been given into his breast pocket. The Palestinian was as jumpy as a cat. 'I'm sorry I couldn't do anything for your friends,' he went on, 'but there was only enough material for you.' Pride of craftsmanship calmed some of Henry's agitation. 'You'll find a passport there, properly stamped,' he announced, 'a travel warrant, also stamped, and a couple of letters. You're Mario Brioni, sir. That's if you want to be an I-ty. I'd better go now, sir. Good luck.' He shook hands with Natusch, gave Frank and Joob a half-bow, and left.

The New Zealander passed the little folder to his two friends without a word and stayed on the alert whilst they examined it. The verdict came quickly. 'It's perfect,' Frank said slowly. His eyes were wide with admiration. 'This is first-class work.' Joob Sengor, taking longer over his examination, agreed, and with that, Natusch was really satisfied. Joob was a protégé of the great Bentinck, and a connoisseur of forgery. He put the documents back into his pocket and breathed thanks once again to the ever-helpful Henry Lowenstein.

CHAPTER TWELVE

HUNTERS AND QUARRY

NATUSCH had made allowance for most of the pitfalls which could lie ahead, but for all his thinking he had overlooked a vital point; and the last item in the planning was done for him by Lowenstein.

All this manoeuvring was essential. The Gestapo at the crowded Buda prison hadn't bothered to make a photo and fingerprint check with the Berlin files, which could identify everyone who had ever been captured, but the Neubrandenberg authorities could hardly be expected to repeat this mistake. It was too much to ask.

It meant that Natusch couldn't risk facing the new interrogators. He'd have to jump off the train – if he could – somewhere *en route* to the Oflag, dodge the resultant hue and cry, and change his identity from Edouard van Hootegem to Mario Brioni, an Italian who happened to be travelling legitimately, and on the same stretch of line, but in the opposite direction from Stettin to Hegyshalom near the Hungarian border. Stettin lay thirty miles east of Neubrandenberg, which made the revised journey feasible.

So far, so good, but – there were substantial 'buts'. Supposing the luck failed and he were to be arrested before he got to Hegyshalom? And supposing some bright Hun then checked and found there was no such person as Mario Brioni? If that happened he'd have to admit – he could hardly reveal his real name – that he was van Hootegem, the Dutchman who couldn't speak Dutch, which would be enough to spark off a really intensive enquiry. Natusch knew what would follow. The Berlin files would at last be consulted, and would announce loud and clear that Corporal Natusch, alias van Hootegem, alias Brioni, was back once again in the Fatherland; and with a multiple identity like that to intrigue them, it was a safe bet that the Gestapo would put in an early appearance.

He was feeling depressed about it, and for once a bit lost, when Henry Lowenstein came in with the rations and played yet another trump card on his behalf. 'You could be me, sir,' he suggested. Natusch looked up blankly and waited for an explanation. The guard was some distance away. 'Yes, you could be me,' Henry repeated. 'If you get arrested.' He gave one of his rare smiles. 'I mean the real Henry Lowenstein. My name's Lewis here. Henry Lewis. When the Germans were questioning us at Szigetvar, I remembered that recaptured prisoners get a month in jail, so I gave them a lot of wrong answers. Said I'd jumped off one of their prisons trains going from Greece to Germany a couple of years back, and that I'd been in Hungary ever since. I had to give a wrong name, of course. It means now that my real identity's vacant, and so far as I can see, no one's going to claim it. It's yours, sir, if you'd like it.' He groped under his shirt collar. 'Look, here's my British Army disc. That should convince anyone.'

Natusch jumped at Henry's offer. He took the identity disc, slipped it round his neck, and with the guard still absent, asked and memorized the few details that were necessary to the deception. He was thankful that this time they didn't involve much more than name, rank and number. And with his second line of defence now secure, and a double allowance made against human failure, he relaxed. With care and planning of this order, once he won free again, *nothing* could go wrong.

Frank Brackel, Joob Sengor and Roy Natusch left Stalag 17A next day. They travelled north, spent the night uncomfortably in a prison cell in Vienna, and next morning, with alert guards watching for a wrong move, entrained again. The party, three guards and three prisoners, was still intact ten hours later. By then, they had left Vienna some hundreds of miles to the south, Czechoslovakia was hours down the line, and Breslau lay a mere twenty or thirty miles ahead. It was growing dark, and once again, as Natusch leaned back in his corner seat, the familiar tingle that was half fear and half eagerness crept through him.

Quite suddenly it became a near-agony for him to sit quietly. He wanted to stand, to shake his shoulders, to let the repressed sighs and shivers out, but he remained still. The three guards opposite were relaxed and tired with their long journey, but alertness could return at the snap of a finger: and for the break that was now at hand, he reckoned he would need every fractional part of three seconds. It would be touch and go even then.

He gave Frank Brackel a prearranged nudge as the train moved away slowly from the small station that was their last stop before Breslau. If he were to escape at all, it had to be now, before they gathered speed. It was unlikely that there would be another chance. Next morning, the last lap of the journey would be on the Breslau–Berlin express, in daytime, and in a corridor coach, with Neubrandenberg a mere seventy miles farther on.

Frank glanced up, nodded imperceptibly, and then froze as the carriage glided past a group of policemen standing at the end of the platform. What they were doing there on a deserted railway station at that time of the evening was inexplicable; but they couldn't have been worse placed. Natusch had intended to jump there, had banked on having a level six feet or so of landing ground free of even a casual porter or passenger, and he would have jumped with the train doing no more that 15 m.p.h. He waited about five seconds in an agony of indecision before nudging Frank again. The train was now going appreciably faster, and its speed increasing, but he had no option. They were due to stay the night in Breslau – probably in a police cell – and there would be no further chance of escape.

Frank leaned forward to mask his movements. Natusch found time to squeeze his arm, to say briefly. 'Good luck, Frank,' and then the plan snapped into action. He jerked the door open and swung out and down on to the carriage step almost in one movement. A blast of cold air hit him immediately and did its best to loosen a precarious grip on the hand-rail, but he held on. It was dark now. Below him was a black void that gave no clue to the kind of surface he'd land on. He leapt outwards as startled shouts came from the German guards.

The landing didn't hurt him; nor was he aware then of the high cost that was being demanded for it. Something struck his left leg just above the knee sufficiently hard to turn what should have been a controlled slither into an untidy cartwheel landing that was all arms and legs flying everywhere. He escaped mutilation under the fast-turning wheels, skidded helplessly along the rough track, and was knocked out as his head thudded into some loose rubble. He came to almost immediately, and was up and away with the clitter-clatter of wheels still loud in his ears.

Unseen signal wires tripped him as he crossed the track towards the far embankment. The search would be less keen on this side of the railroad. He got up a second time, and as he did, it occurred to him that he'd lost his civilian hat. For some reason – Natusch couldn't fathom what it was – it seemed important to retrieve it, and still dazed, he walked back along the permanent way. He found the hat. It was lying on the track not far from the iron stake upon which he'd come very near to impaling himself. He jammed it on his head clumsily, crossed the rails again, slid down an embankment, and walked through a clump of trees towards what he hoped would be a path or a minor road.

The plan was simple. He intended to travel cross-country through the night, strike another railway line, and when morning came, or the morning after, if necessary, resume Mario Brioni's interrupted journey to Hegyshalom. It was a straightforward scheme that didn't involve real difficulty. He had a valid passport, a travel warrant which covered the lines in this locality, more German marks than he needed – the American dollars had seen to that – and he could speak Italian well enough to confound any tinpot *bahnhof* Fuehrer who might take it into his head to desert his own tongue and try his ally's.

Natusch smiled at the way the plan was working out, and as he did, a queer taste came to his lips. He stopped and brought up a questing hand. It came down smeared with blood, but there was something besides that. His left thumb was out of joint. He looked at it blankly, felt it, tried to pull it back into place with the other hand, but it, too, seemed to have suffered in the crash landing. He hadn't enough strength. He felt his head gingerly, ran the good hand – or at least, the better hand – over his hair, and found it wet and a trifle sticky. A sudden weakness came, a feeling of nausea that forced him to lie down on the damp grass with his senses reeling: but he wasn't given time to recover properly. Mosquitoes got the blood scent, and came in eager hordes to speed him on his way. He heeded them, and set off across open country, searching now not so much for a road as for a stream where he might bathe his head and face. Mario Brioni, he remembered, would need to look presentable tomorrow morning when he was buying his railway ticket.

For a brief while, the *joie de vivre* and ebullience which follow a successful escape returned to lighten Natusch's step, but it didn't last long. He kept falling over unaccountably, and even slight unevenness of the ground seemed enough to trip him. He kept going, but it was an effort.

The stream was a mile away. Natusch heard it rippling and burbling a welcome, and fell over twice as he descended the steep bank. It was then that his left leg decided to call it a day. He sat where he had fallen, ran a hand down the outside of his trouser leg, found the hole that had been ripped in it, and probed about inside. His fingers seemed to stick just above the knee, and the leg grew sore. The iron bar had torn a great gash in his thigh.

He lay back, aware, suddenly and yet dispassionately, that this was the end. Luck had failed him after all. He couldn't go on, couldn't keep his appointment with the morning train, couldn't negotiate the unauthorized but easy border crossing that would see him back into Hungary, nor manage the much easier rail journey which would take him back to his friends in Budapest. He was too badly battered. He had a leg out of action, a dislocated thumb and a bloody head that was still bleeding, and the injuries were too severe for him to have any hope of returning to Hegyshalom by train. By tomorrow, every railway station for miles around would be on the alert for an escaped Dutchman – probably cut and dishevelled – and if he were to go near a *Bahnhof* now, it would be tantamount to surrender.

He got up, waded carefully into the stream and began bathing his wounds. He tried once again to correct the dislocated thumb, but failed, and resumed the bathing. His head had cleared now and thinking was easier. He had already realized that he would have to give himself up. There was no option. He couldn't travel by train, but equally, in his present condition, he couldn't get far on foot. It would be as well, too, if something were done about the hurt leg. He waded back to the edge of the stream, waited until a sudden faintness had passed, and continued thinking.

The escape attempt, upon which so much depended, was over almost before it had begun, and only the reckoning remained. That much was clear: but there might still be a way to adjust the bill in his favour.

He decided to head away from the railway altogether, to put as much distance between it and him as possible. If he could manage to keep going during the night and reach a village about six or seven miles away by morning, he could give himself up there as Henry Lowenstein, escaped prisoner from Stalag VIIIB at Lamsdorf, and perhaps get the hurts attended to. It seemed unlikely that isolated villages would be notified about the escaped Dutchman, but even if they were, the Lowenstein alias and the Lowenstein identity tag should lull suspicion. A phone call to the Stalag would confirm that Lowenstein *had* escaped from there, and at this stage at least, his British Army identification disc would hardly be questioned.

Natusch felt less happy about how he'd explain his injuries – other than he'd fallen off a lorry – or his long absence from the Stalag, until he remembered that there was no need to tell anyone anything beyond name, rank and number. If he could manage to get himself returned to VIIIB at Lamsdorf, which was the obvious place to send him, the S.B.O. there would vouch that he was Henry Lowenstein – he'd do that automatically and ask questions later – and the Germans would believe him, dismiss Natusch as a surly, unco-operative *Lümmel* and send him to prison for the regulation thirty days. They'd have no need to check with the Berlin files, which would mean that as soon as he came out of the cooler, he could merge with the thousands of other prisoners at VIIIB, carry on being Henry Lowenstein, and finally lay the ghosts of both Natusch and van Hootegem. It would be one way of ensuring the safety of those Hungarians whose fate, for all he knew, still depended on his keeping clear of the Gestapo.

There remained Brioni, of course, poor Mario Brioni, who had never been born and who was now dead. His position was impossible. His passport wasn't duplicated in the ubiquitous German records, his travel warrant was faked, and if he were to turn up at a railway station looking as if he'd been in a battle, the Gestapo would be along hot-foot to investigate. No, Mario Brioni, the perfect cover for the train journey to Hegyshalom, was now a potential betrayer. Natusch brought out his passport and travel warrant, and the letter from his *carissima* Emilia, who loved him dearly, and with real regret at having to discard such superb forgeries, hid them under a stone. Mario the Italian, had now gone, and with him the beautiful Emilia, who had poured out her heart. An extract from her letter came to mind, 'Io te amo con tutt' il mio cuore. Sempre. Non lasciame mai, Mario,' it said. 'I love you with all my heart,' she had pleaded, 'for ever. Never leave me, Mario.'

The poignancy of her epitaph and a spasm of pain brought sudden tears to Natusch's eyes. He shook his head in annoyance, and instantly regretted it as more pain came crowding in. He was no longer Mario Brioni, he thought irritably. Damn Brioni. And his Emilia with him. Henceforth, he was Henry Lowenstein, escaped Kriegsgefangener from Lamsdorf, born in Prague, lately, if anyone of importance wanted to know, of 15 Princess Mary Avenue, Tel Aviv, aged forty years, with a British Army identity disc to back him up, and more details that might be in the Lamsdorf files at his command. The age gap between Henry Lowenstein and Roy Natusch didn't worry him. Lowenstein, for all his nervousness, was a young-looking forty; Natusch, what with the alarms and excursions of the past few months, was getting to be an old-looking twenty-five.

He got to his feet again. He was feeling better now. The cold water had closed the jagged cuts in his thigh and head and had checked the bleeding, and if it didn't start again there seemed no reason why he shouldn't cover the seven miles he'd set himself, or even more.

But he was slower than he'd expected. Much slower. He crossed the shallow stream carefully, and continued at little more than snail's pace over open ground away from the railway. He kept going. He didn't know how far he walked, nor for how long, nor how he persuaded the hurt leg to function, but it did, and that was enough. He met no one. After a while, he seemed to lose track of time altogether, but he felt pleased when he saw a light twinkling somewhere far ahead; and exhausted and more than a little lightheaded when he reached it. He dragged himself wearily up some stone steps. Here was refuge, he told himself, here was haven from the Gestapo, somewhere where his hurts would be salved. He collapsed just inside the door.

The full implication of what had happened didn't strike Natusch until later. He hadn't travelled seven miles, nor anything like seven miles, nor had his journey lasted more than a couple of hours. He'd walked in a wide, erratic semi-circle which began at the little stream, a mile from where he'd jumped off the train, and which ended outside the railway station that had been the last stop before Breslau, and where the police standing on the platform had been the unwitting authors of his present troubles.

Someone shook him vigorously. He heard a voice shouting 'Raus! Raus!' and opened his eyes to find himself lying on a wooden bench in the waiting room of the station. It was morning and he felt awful. Above him, one of the three guards who had been escorting them to the Dutch Oflag at Neubrandenberg was gesturing fiercely. 'Get up!' he ordered. 'Fast!' Natusch tried to obey, but he was stiff, and failed badly. He got no credit for trying. The guard grabbed his shoulder, and was wrenching him up when he noticed Natusch's head and the blood-stained trouser leg.

After that, he was surprisingly gentle. He called in a German Red Cross man who put the dislocated thumb right, whistled when he saw the extent of the other damage, but did a workmanlike bandaging job that gave the New Zealander renewed confidence. It was still difficult to walk and no one offered to help, but when he and the guard once again entrained for Breslau, he found that if he swung the hurt leg forward from the hip and got it squarely under him, he was still mobile. So long as he wasn't pushed.

The real test came at Breslau station an hour or so later. There, the N.C.O. went away, leaving a young soldier to guard Natusch, and for four hours, from nine in the morning until an hour past midday, the New Zealander stood on the platform, waiting. He had to stand. There was no place to sit, other than on the ground, and he had a stubborn mood on. Bad leg or no bad leg, he decided, he wasn't going to squat like a damned coolie. Nor ask any favours. Inwardly, deep down, he hoped that one of these Huns would have the grace to bring him a chair, or a stool, and maybe a drink of some sort as well, but none did.

He grew more stubborn and more determined as the hours wore on. He was now looking the worse for wear again. The cut on his head had reopened, and blood trickling down his forehead had caked on his eyebrow and had set hard on his cheek. It was uncomfortable, like shaving lather that has gone stiff, but discomfort wasn't a serious issue. His leg wound had also reopened. The bandages were bloodstained and there were dark smears on the platform.

He stayed where he was, not moving lest the gesture should be interpreted as an appeal for help. For four hours swarms of German civilians passed by, some curious, some stealing surreptitious glances, some looking frankly concerned, but none doing anything about it, until towards noon, when a young girl brought him a glass of water. He was still on his feet when the N.C.O. returned. He seemed surprised to find his prisoner standing. 'You all right?' he asked. He didn't wait for an answer. 'Hospital's waiting for you,' he added briskly. 'Come on. Let's go.'

By this time Natusch couldn't walk at all. It was as much as he could do to stand, but the German was a sensible man. A moment later Natusch found himself being marched at a quick pace towards the station exit, with one arm around the guard's neck, the other around the burly young soldier who had stayed with him, and his feet making no more than token contact with the ground. He fainted before they had gone ten paces.

It was three days before he was conscious again. He opened his eyes, became aware, vaguely, of a French orderly fussing over him, and as the mists cleared, of a doctor who was strapping his leg to an iron plate. He kept the plate for several weeks. For a while it was touch and go whether or not he'd be permanently lame, and at one time the leg itself was in danger, but once he began to mend, he improved fast.

A month's stay at Breslau hospital saw Natusch back in fair shape. The fierce gash in his leg hadn't quite healed, but he could walk well enough with the aid of a stick, and by now his head was almost wholly mended. It left him with a zigzag scar as a memento of his second and, he hoped, last leap from a moving train, and so far as he knew, the wits below the scar were in good fettle, which was as well. He was soon to need them.

His Dutch nationality had now overridden all the proposed changes. The German guard who had found him had recognized him instantly as van Hootegem, which meant that Henry Lowenstein's patient effort and craftsmanship had been in vain. Even his army disc had become a risky thing to carry around. Natusch got rid of it, and in doing so abandoned yet another identity which should have solved his problems for him.

On 2nd August, 1944, two guards arrived from the Dutch Oflag at Neubrandenberg to collect their missing prisoner, and within the hour the little party was thundering northwards on the Stettin express. There wasn't much conversation during the journey. Escape was out of the question, and Natusch sat quietly in a corner seat, concentrating on the best tactics to employ once he reached Neubrandenberg, and checking his memory against all the details which Frank Brackel had given him. It seemed certain that at best he'd be fighting a delaying action. His Hungarian civil papers were in order, and the camp authorities would know that the Gestapo had passed him as Eddie van Hootegem, but the bugbear of the language difficulty remained.

The Wehrmacht, of course, were on a sure winner. They had only to check his fingerprints and it would be goodbye to further deception. The Gestapo would then be notified that the alleged Dutch lieutenant whom they'd sent from Budapest to Neubrandenberg Oflag, and who had tried to escape *en route*, was in reality a New Zealand corporal named Roy Natusch: but as always, one last chance remained. According to Frank Brackel, official messages from one Service to the other usually took a month in delivery. Even then the Gestapo might not pounce right away ... It didn't sound very comforting.

A Hauptmann was waiting for him at the Oflag. He harangued Natusch in fluent Dutch, overrode his protests, and asked several questions in quick succession before the New Zealander could make his voice heard. 'I don't understand you,' he said for the third time. He spoke loudly. 'Ich verstehe nicht, Herr Hauptmann. I speak English, not Dutch. You'll need an interpreter.'

The Hauptmann was another officer of the old school. He gave a start, looked at his prisoner disbelievingly for a moment, and then switched to English. 'Who are you?' he demanded. 'Are you English?' Natusch told him No. 'I am Edouard van Hootegem,' he said. 'First Lieutenant, the Royal Netherlands Army. Number 155501.' The Hauptmann betrayed his astonishment. 'You tell me,' he said incredulously, 'that you belong to the Dutch Army and yet you cannot speak Dutch? And I am to believe this?'

The next half-hour was a repeat performance of the Gestapo interrogation. Natusch told the Hauptmann the same carefully thought-out story that he'd given before, told it fluently, and with plenty of detail. The Hauptmann, sitting well back in his chair and nodding from time to time, listened. His big guns were trained but not yet fired. 'I think,' he said, as Natusch finished, 'that you would have done well to have stayed in Australia. But since you are here—' he dropped the air of mock sympathy '—you can now tell me how you got here.' There was an edge to his voice. 'With dates and details, please.'

The Hauptmann wasn't to know that this was precisely the line which Natusch was hoping he would take. It was an obvious testing ground that Frank Brackel and he had been over a dozen times until he knew every last detail. He'd been demobilized, he said, by the Wehrmacht in the autumn of 1940, summoned to their Amsterdam H.Q. in July '42, arrested, and sent by train to Nuremberg Langwasser. His next stop, he went on, was the Dutch camp at Stanislau in Poland. He was about to move on from there when the Hauptmann held up his hand. 'We will stay a while,' he said, 'and compare notes.' A half-smile was playing over the German's face. 'It so happens that I was at Stanislau Oflager myself. I know it, therefore, equally as well as you do. Tell me—' his voice became crisp again '—who was the senior Dutch general?'

Natusch didn't hesitate. Stanislau Oflager was another of his strong points. He gave the Dutch general's name, described him, and in the same unconcerned voice, added the names of two or three high-ranking officers. It impressed the Hauptmann, but it didn't satisfy him. In quick succession, he demanded a sketch of the camp, asked Natusch to plot three escape tunnels which had been discovered and filled in, to describe his own quarters, and to name various camp activities.

The New Zealander passed all four tests. By now he was beginning to wonder why this persevering Intelligence officer didn't take his fingerprints and have done with it, but he didn't get time to ponder. 'And your own escape from

Stanislau,' the Hauptmann went on. He paused to light his pipe. 'How did you manage that?'

Natusch took his matches, uninvited, found a cigarette and lit it. His hands were steady. 'I jumped out of a railway carriage,' he replied. He stopped and damped the cigarette carefully where it was burning too fast. 'It was January '44 – I forget the exact date – but you should know. The whole camp was being taken back to Germany. It was—' he added, to show that there was plenty of detail available '—number three train, it was a Sunday, and it was snowing hard. Remember?'

The Hauptmann, for all his professional distrust, was very nearly convinced. It was the first time he'd ever dealt with a Dutch Army officer who didn't know his own language, but the story he'd just heard was too detailed and too accurate, by his own knowledge, to be faked. The Gestapo had passed it, too, which was a pointer. *They* weren't easily satisfied, and had their own methods of checking and double-checking their informants. He looked at Natusch again and played his trump card. 'What is my name?' he said suddenly. Natusch was ready for him. He'd never seen this German before in his life, but he'd said himself that he'd been at Stanislau, and Frank Brackel had described each of the six camp officers minutely. There seemed a sporting chance that he might yet avoid being fingerprinted. 'You're Hauptmann Schmidt,' he said. He stubbed out the cigarette. 'From No. 2 compound. I'm surprised you don't remember me.'

That clinched it. The Intelligence officer closed the file in front of him and leaned back in his chair. 'That is all, Lieutenant,' he said. He gave a thin smile. 'You are a remarkable man. And you will now go to prison for thirty days. As you know, it is the regulation punishment given to escapers who are recaptured. You will observe—' the German's quiet humour asserted itself '—that we do not punish you for your escape.'

Natusch wasn't concerned at the prison sentence. Thirty days was nothing, detracted nothing from the wholly unexpected achievement of being accepted once again as van Hootegem. He went into gaol there and then, but friends were watching. Frank Brackel smuggled in magazines and extra food, his tobacco wasn't confiscated, and for once prison life was almost luxurious; but a sting was coming up fast. On the seventh day, Hauptmann Schmidt came into the cell. He ignored a cheerful 'Good afternoon' and when he spoke there was no trace of his previous tolerance. 'You are not Lieutenant van Hootegem,' he said blandly. 'Unless you give me your correct name, now, and explain the reason for this impersonation, I intend to hand you back to the Gestapo.'

He stood watching, waiting for a reaction to his ultimatum, but Natusch didn't lose his composure. Somehow – this much was obvious – Schmidt had discovered that he *was* an impostor, and his threat of the Gestapo was very real, but there was no need to give in at the first crack of the whip. There was just an outside chance that he was bluffing, was making one last check. Natusch decided to test his bluff before going to the confession stool. 'But I don't understand you,' he said. 'I *am* Edouard van Hootegem. You know that. I told you all about myself a few days back. What makes you come here now and say I'm not?'

Natusch wasn't meant to sleep that night. In the early hours a *Gefreiter* and two *Soldaten* unlocked the door of his cell, led him out to what was probably a German Black Maria, but what at that hour looked more like a tumbril, and without a word being spoken, drove off. Natusch remembered the Hauptmann's cold hostility, and the thought came to him that 2 a.m. is as good a time as any for a quiet disposal job, but his fear was unfounded. The vehicle kept comfortingly to the main road, ignored the dark anonymity of the byways, and drew up outside the main Wehrmacht barracks on the hill above Neubrandenberg.

He stayed in this barracks for another week. The new cell was again comfortable, but his peace of mind was now shattered, and solitary imprisonment regained a good deal of its old malice. He didn't know where he stood. He didn't know what had happened to the real Eddie van Hootegem either, although he feared that Eddie must have been recaptured, and he had no idea how much or how little Hauptmann Schmidt really knew. Nor whether or not the German would carry out his Gestapo threat if he didn't get a confession. Natusch *did* know that at all costs he had to keep clear of the S.S. and now that his identity was being actively challenged, the thought occurred that it might be as well to forestall the inevitable fingerprint check by telling Schmidt all he wanted to know. Not quite all, of course. If he could convince the Hauptmann that his aim all along had been the innocuous one of covering van Hootegem's own escape, so much the better. It would label him as a stooge, and would mean that he'd be returned to a British camp, possibly 184 at Wolfsberg where he'd come from, with, hopefully, a month's start over any Gestapo pursuit.

But the musing came to nothing. Hauptmann Schmidt had already been superseded. Next morning an *Unteroffizier* and a guard escorted Natusch to the Camp Kommandant's office, and with a good deal of heel-clicking and 'Jawohl, Herr Kommandant', showed him in.

The Kommandant was sitting behind a huge desk. He was a bald-headed, weatherbeaten man of about fifty, and he was a full colonel. At his side, stiff and hostile, stood Hauptmann Schmidt. In front, seated on chairs, were Frank Brackel and the Dutch adjutant. Natusch swung forward on his stick, saluted the German colonel, and then shook hands with Frank Brackel. 'Glad to see you, Frank!' he said. 'How goes it?' There was no play-acting about the greeting. Frank gripped his hand, introduced him to his senior officer, and as the guard brought a chair, managed one all-important gesture. 'Don't bluff,' it signalled. 'Or you're sunk.'

The colonel was in no hurry. He lit a cigarette, handed one to Natusch, and waited until they'd both savoured the first few puffs before he got down to business. 'You have come here as Lieutenant van Hootegem of the Dutch Army,' he said. 'But you are not van Hootegem. If you persist in saying you are, I will send you back to the Gestapo and ask them for confirmation. If you give me your true identity, and it concerns the Wehrmacht, I will keep you here at Neubrandenberg until we get confirmation from Berlin. If they say you are a genuine prisoner-of-war, you will be treated accordingly.' The Colonel spoke without rancour. 'Is that clear?'

The issue was crystal clear. Natusch hesitated a moment or two, to show that he didn't panic at the mention of the word 'Gestapo', and then looked squarely at the colonel. 'I think you already know who I am, sir,' he said. It seemed best not to waste words. 'My name is Natusch. Corporal Roy Spencer Natusch of the New Zealand Army. Pay number 33965. P.O.W. 7456. I was originally at Stalag 18A at Wolfsberg.' He was careful to retain the non-commissioned rank. Getting back to Wolfsberg, if he could manage it, was only half the battle. To have a sporting chance of another escape, he would also have to get out on a working party of his own choice.

The Kommandant was smiling. He didn't ask, because it wouldn't have been ethical to do so, but he seemed to have accepted that Natusch had swapped identities with van Hootegem to aid some dubious scheme of the Dutchman. He didn't delve into that question, possibly because he felt that there was already enough unsaid and likely to remain unsaid to be going on with, and possibly because ethics once again intervened; but it was patent that he was no fool. Natusch, watching him, kept his feelings under tight control. If his present surmise was correct, he was safe; but there was always the chance of a trap. He drew on his cigarette, examined it, and looked up unconcerned. Exchanging identities, which was all that he'd tacitly admitted to, was after all a minor offence.

The Colonel gave his verdict indirectly. 'So you are a New Zealander,' he mused. He looked thoughtful. 'You had better be. Where were you first captured?' Natusch answered him truthfully. 'At Kalamai, in Greece, sir. In April 1941.' The German's interest quickened. 'So?' he observed. 'I was in Greece too, also in 1941. Were you at Napleion? We had some hard fighting there.'

Natusch did nothing to shorten the conversation which followed. He discussed what he knew of the British retreat with the Kommandant, and mentioned how he and other engineers had mined the roads all along the east coast from Corinth as far south as Tripolos, only to be cut off by Wehrmacht spearheads who had raced down the unguarded roads on the west coast. The German Colonel saw the humour of that at once, and laughed uproariously. 'I know,' he beamed. 'That would be your Intelligence people. We have them too. They've done the same kind of thing for us. Still, we all make mistakes in wartime.' He looked at Natusch keenly. 'It is to be hoped that you're not making one now. You haven't told me why you were impersonating a Dutch officer, but I won't press it. The Wehrmacht do not use force to gain information.' He spoke briefly to Hauptmann Schmidt before going on. 'I'm keeping you here for the time being. As soon as I've had your photograph and fingerprints confirmed, I shall send you back to Wolfsberg. No doubt you have friends there. In the meantime—' the bluff Colonel smiled '—you may retain officer status and rations.'

The New Zealander stayed two more weeks at the Dutch Oflag before going back to Wolfsberg. In some ways it was a pleasant fortnight, and certainly should have been the most entertaining of his whole captivity, but despite privileges and the unexpected camaraderie of German guards, he spent much of the time in a private hell of his own making. He didn't know whether or not the Gestapo had been told about the van Hootegem–Natusch identity switch, and he couldn't be sure that they weren't even now on his trail. He tried hard to put the whole thing out of his mind, and at times succeeded. Especially outside the camp. He was now allowed escorted walks, and on these, in bright daylight, fear of the Gestapo burnt low – but there were the nights. . . .

Natusch went for many of these long walks. He roamed far and wide with his escorts, ostensibly seeing more and yet more of the delightful scenery around the Oflag, and in reality strengthening his leg for the escape that was still to be made. He could get along at a fair pace now, but he had to use a stick. He couldn't run, and that troubled him. In the past, his legs had been good friends, and there was the possibility that their major test was yet to come.

His stamina improved fast. His left leg, the one which had been ripped open by the iron bar, was weak, but by some miracle it had escaped permanent injury. The bar had gouged a huge hole, but it had missed the arteries and sinews and had done damage that time had shown to be spectacular rather than serious. At the hospital at Breslau, the doctors had thought that he'd chipped his shinbone into the bargain, but if he had, it didn't seem to matter. Good food and plenty of walking combined to make him strong again and to pump back some of the old zip and acceleration into his feet.

But he had only a fortnight of this pampered existence, and with thoughts of the Gestapo for ever harrying his peace of mind, even a fortnight was too long. When the Wolfsberg guards eventually arrived, Natusch was as glad to see them as he'd yet been to see German soldiers.

CHAPTER THIRTEEN

THE BRIGAND

THE journey south was uneventful. The two guards were amiable characters, and their first call, as soon as the local train from Neubrandenberg reached Berlin, was to a *Gasthaus* nearby for three pint handles of lager. They boarded the Vienna express, and Natusch, who had been on it before, didn't think that this leg of the long journey would be completed in a day. He found himself agreeably mistaken. It was a crack train, and the German railwaymen, with their Fuehrer's latest slogan 'the wheels must roll for victory' to spur them on, were on their mettle.

He spent the night in a military jail in Vienna, and the following morning boarded a local train that was pure Emmett compared with the sleek Berlin–Vienna express, and resumed the journey south to Wolfsberg. Once again, Natusch gave no thought to escaping. He wouldn't have gone if a dozen opportunities had occurred instead of the inevitable one or two which did present themselves. These guards were taking him to the very place he wanted to reach.

The little train puffed into Wolfsberg station somewhere around noon and discharged about a dozen passengers. Half an hour later Natusch walked through the Stalag gates, with his brief respite at an end. Grim reality quickly replaced it. This was Wolfsberg, Stalag 18A, and it had already given him – in unmistakable terms – a month's notice to quit.

His first hour in the camp wasn't a happy one. There wasn't a soul there he knew, and he got nothing but ill-disguised hostility until he spotted Captain Beatty, a New Zealand medical officer. That changed the picture completely, and also staved off some wholly unexpected unpleasantness. The captain took him to the camp leader, R.S.M. Stephenson, told him they'd known each other for some time at another camp at Spittal-um-der-Drau, and vouched for the New Zealander's integrity. In doing so, he scotched a rumour already travelling around 18A that the new man was a German *agent provocateur*.

Possibly that was a nearer escape from bad trouble than Natusch realized; but it was an escape for all that, and as if to make up for it, the going was now easy. With Captain Beatty and R.S.M Stephenson firmly on his side, the help he needed came fast. He told them his history, explained that the Gestapo might very soon be gunning for him, and left the problem of departure to them.

They responded well. The R.S.M. took Joe Gretton, the man in charge of working parties, to one side, told him that the new arrival might have to leave fast, and that the danger signal would be a request by anyone for his file from the German administrative office. Gretton worked in this office, and was the one man in the camp who would know immediately if such a request was made. That was good fast work by R.S.M. Stephenson, which solved half of the new problem. It was left to Captain Beatty to tackle the more delicate part.

Captain Beatty's task was to contact, or at least to locate, one of the anti-Hitler Austrians of whom reference had been made at Wolfsberg, at Szigetvar and no doubt at many other camps near the Hungarian and Yugoslav borders, and to persuade him to sponsor an escape. Both Captain Beatty and Natusch were convinced that these people did exist. Many of the old families in both countries were related to the Austrian aristocracy, and if rumour had any basis at all, it seemed certain that there *were* anti-Hitler Austrians about – if you could find them. Natusch was fortunate that Captain Beatty shared this view, and doubly so when, two days later, he produced – it seemed out of a hat – a fellow New Zealander named Dick Nancarrow who had actually worked for one.

'He's a count,' Nancarrow said. 'A real Jerry. You know the type. Big fat fellow with a bullet head and no neck and a shaving brush in his hat. But he's all right. I worked on his estate at Radkersburg, about three miles from the Hungarian border, and we got on fine. He's a director of an armaments firm somewhere, but the Gestapo don't trust him. They've been after him twice already. He speaks English, too.' Nancarrow looked at Natusch enigmatically. In this life, you didn't enquire too deeply into possible escape attempts. 'If you're thinking of anything,' he hazarded, 'a move, maybe, and you contact this joker, he'll fix you up all right. Personal attention guaranteed.'

The New Zealander's star seemed now very much in the ascendant. He thank Dick Nancarrow, arranged with the R.S.M. and Joe Gretton to be included in the next *Arbeit* party, and with that, relaxed, knowing that he'd done all he could do to keep events moving. There was nothing for it now but to wait.

A free and easy ten days went by before the alarm sounded. Natusch's nerve grew strong again, his leg improved still further with continued good food and exercise, and every day Joe Gretton came to assure him that no one had yet been making enquiries about Corporal Natusch. On the tenth day, Gretton worked late and didn't make his visit until well after dark. It was obvious that he was agitated. 'The balloon's gone up, Roy,' he said tersely. 'A Gestapo chap got here this afternoon, and he's been nosing around ever since. Smooth character, name of Greuber. He's still here. That's what kept me late. He's going back to Vienna tomorrow, and he's taking your file with him.' Gretton looked sombre. 'If I were you,' he advised, 'I'd get outa here quick. Want me to fix it?'

Natusch accepted the offer very fast indeed. The Gestapo agent's visit meant that he now had between two days and a week's grace before the arresting party arrived. There was no longer any doubt that they *would* arrive, and he didn't want to be around to meet them. 'Get me out tomorrow, Joe, if you can,' he said. He drew a finger across his throat bleakly. 'Do your best.'

Joe Gretton proved equal to the occasion. Next day, a hurriedly assembled Radkersburg *Arbeit* party marched out of the Stalag gates hours too early, as usual, waited patiently until the train drew in, and then settled down to enjoy the trip. Natusch didn't take much notice of it. He was wearing civilian clothes under his uniform, he had compass, map and money concealed in a Red Cross food parcel, two letters in an inside pocket, and some apprehension in his mind as to whether Herr Greuber had won too big a start.

Dick Nancarrow had written both letters. One, which had no superscription, was to the anti-Hitler count-cum-armaments-director, and the other to Ginger Jones, an English P.O.W. who worked on the Count's estate. Both letters said much the same thing – that Roy Natusch was a genuine New Zealander, not a Gestapo agent, that he had to cross the border fast, and that he'd need help to do so. Natusch found himself wondering whether the help thus solicited would be enough, and in time.

Radkersburg was the sleepy back-of-beyond place that Dick Nancarrow had pictured. It was a little Austrian village squatting on the banks of the Mur River, with rich fertile country all around it, peaceful, somnolent, and with only the presence of frontier guards to give a reminder of the war that was soon to overtake it. The Hungarian border lay a bare three miles to the north-east, but the other frontier, the Yugoslav one, was much nearer. It lay on the village's own doorstep, on the far side of the bridge spanning the Mur, which like Browning's Weser was deep and wide, and which made a formidable barrier against illegal crossings. In daytime, the bridge over it was unpatrolled and the local people came and went as they pleased; but when darkness fell, it was different. From then until dawn, guards manned machine-gun posts on the Yugoslav side of the river, and one crossed at one's peril.

The topography of Radkersburg was simple. The frontier guards were billeted in the southern part of the village, near the bridge, the prisoners' lager was in the centre, and somewhere on the outskirts lay the home of the embittered man who could ease a journey out of Reich territory – if he chose to.

Natusch met Ginger Jones that evening. He was a stocky, determined-looking chap with friendly eyes and the expected rich thatch that had earned him his nickname. The New Zealander liked him on sight, so much so that he held back none of his hopes or fears, but told him everything. Ginger listened attentively. The Count, he said, was at home, which was a piece of extraordinary good fortune. He'd got back only last night from a long trip, and was due to go away again in a few days' time for an even longer duration. It meant that if he agreed to sponsor an escape, and, as Ginger stressed, that was very far from certain, the three of them would have to work fast to accomplish it.

Natusch decided to write a note to the Count, to give him more background than Dick Nancarrow's letter had done, and also to add a personal touch to the appeal which was being made. He did so, and found himself both annoyed and concerned at not being able to strike the right note, at not conveying adequately the urgency of his appeal. 'So you will understand, sir—' the letter ended '—that I must leave here tomorrow or the day after. I daren't stay longer. I leave it to you, Herr Count, to decide whether you will help me, and if you will, which route to take. And once again, I will be more than grateful. . . .'

The next morning, a taciturn guard escorted the New Zealander to the farm where he was to work. The German took him to the house, introduced him briefly to two sad-looking women who, it seemed, owned the place, and that done, stamped out and left the three of them to get on together as best they could.

His departure was abrupt and embarrassing, and for a few moments, the women and Natusch stared foolishly at each other. He knew very little about them. Their husbands, both Wehrmacht men, were somewhere on the Russian Front, but it seemed that there had been no word for a long time, and the obvious conclusion had been drawn, which accounted for the sad looks. The two women were also desperately poor, but they didn't lack for shrewdness. After the initial near-impasse, they looked again at their visitor, this time weighing up his capabilities as a worker. Neither of them seemed impressed.

'Can you milk?' It was the younger one who spoke. Natusch looked at her and said 'Nein.' The last thing he wanted was to land himself with a job that had set times to it. 'Can you scyth?' He gave the Frau another 'Nein', and she tried once again. 'Can you plough?' The woman heaved a sigh as Natusch shook his head a third time. 'You'll learn,' she said shortly. Then, with obvious curiosity, 'What did you do before you were a soldier?'

Natusch waited until the other woman looked up before he answered. He hadn't admitted to a knowledge of farming because he wanted to – had to – establish an immediate ascendancy over both of them. Now was the time to do it, or at least to try. 'Ich bin ein Baumeister,' he said. He spoke coldly and distinctly.

The effect of his statement was immediate. The two women gazed at him with sudden respect. They were peasants, living close to the soil, tilling their few fields, working like slaves from childhood to the grave for very little return. To them, a *Baumeister*, an architect, was someone from another world, a person to whom they would defer naturally and without question. In one inspired moment Natusch found himself graduated from hired help to honoured guest.

He took advantage of the two women, which was mean but necessary. In one day – two at the most – he had to get them accustomed to aloofness on his part, and more important, to sudden and unexplained absences. He began by refusing to eat inside the farmhouse. It was dirty, he said, a hovel unfit for *Herren* to enter. He sat down on a log outside, accepted a cider cup that was brought to him, and promptly handed it back to be washed. It was an impressive start, which set the tone for the rest of the day. By the time it ended and the escort returned, Natusch had managed to establish a class distinction between him and the two women almost equal to that between squire and serf. He had also been away from the farm twice, the second time for over an hour, and no questions had been asked. If the promised help was coming, there'd be no hindrance to it from the farm.

Back at the lager, he found Ginger Jones waiting with the Count's reply to the two letters. Ginger was smiling broadly. 'You're on,' he announced. He made a thumbs-up gesture. 'The old boy's all for you. Read this!'

Natusch read the typewritten message carefully. It was in English, it began and ended abruptly and named no names, which was to be expected, and as Ginger had inferred, it promised help on a princely scale. Budapest could be ruled out, the Count had written. A railway trip to the Hungarian capital called for good papers and passes, which Natusch hadn't got, and which he, the Count, couldn't obtain in time. The alternative, joining the Partisans, was a much sounder idea. The Count approved it wholeheartedly, the more so because one of Tito's political agents happened to be in Radkersburg at that moment, and was willing to co-operate in arranging the escape.

The Austrian sponsor had already thought up a plan which was bold and which displayed a considerable expertise.

On the morrow, he instructed, Natusch was to leave his farm at three o'clock precisely, meet Ginger Jones at a rendezvous, change into civilian clothes and then cross the Mur bridge on foot. Ginger would act as guide as far as the Count's wine-cellars on the Yugoslav side of the Mur, where he had frequent business. There, a local youth would take over and carry on to another rendezvous where two bicycles would be hidden. He and Natusch were to use the bicycles to cover the remaining ten miles or so to a point where the political agent would be waiting. The agent, in his turn, was to act as guide and escort over the last lap of the journey to the Partisans.

Natusch enthused over the Count's scheme. It was neat, it seemed foolproof – he crossed his fingers hurriedly – and he could see nothing in it that would point a finger of suspicion at anyone: least of all, at his poor, husbandless employers.

He awoke early next morning, feeling a peculiar this-is-it optimisim that he couldn't recollect having experienced before. It was Tuesday, 12th September, 1944. It was also a bright sunny morning, warm even at this hour, and full of promise and good omen, that not even the ever-present fear of a sudden Gestapo swoop could subdue.

He reached the farm at 7 a.m. The two sad-eyed women, Frau Berta and Frau Hilde, greeted him with respectful 'Grussgotts' and were pleased and flattered when Natusch raised his cap and gave them a half-bow. That done, he tossed a nod to the guard, took off his jacket and began work.

He worked hard. By noon he had done the best part of a day's stint, and at 2 p.m. he called Hilde and Berta over, showed them various minor repairs which he had done in excess of the day's commitments, and asked for a cider. There was some delay whilst a glass was hurriedly scoured for the *Baumeister*, but in due course the drink arrived. Natusch quaffed it, assured the anxious Frauen that it was palatable, and had another which encouraged them to fetch out a special lunch. He thanked them gravely, did justice to it, and at a quarter to three told them that he was going to visit another prisoner at a farm nearby to taste his cider. He got instant assent. 'Ja! Ja!'s' fairly tumbled from the poor women, and a passing but very real pity for them rose in Natusch.

The feeling of sympathy vanished as he reached the little bridge that was his first rendezvous. He was early, and anxious minutes dragged by before Ginger Jones appeared around a bend of the road. Ginger was pushing a handcart, which had its own part in the plan, and was legitimately on his way to the Count's wine-cellars.

Natusch joined him as he drew level, and they marched on for a while without speaking until the road entered a glade. Here Ginger stopped, looked around quickly, and passed over a sack from his handcart. Natusch vanished into the copse, and was away for about three minutes. When he came back, he was wearing full civilian dress with black trousers, faded blue shirt and jersey, and over them, an old waterproof jacket such as local farmers wore. On his feet were civilian shoes. By now, the more alert German police and guards knew what British Army boots looked like, and it seemed silly to ask for trouble.

Ginger was waiting. Natusch gave him a brief 'O.K.', handed over the sack containing his uniform and boots, and waited as the journey resumed. As soon as Ginger was fifty yards ahead, he began tailing him.

The two men kept accurate stations all the way into Radkersburg. Once in the town, Natusch closed the gap to thirty yards, as agreed, and followed Ginger and his trundling handcart until the bridge came into sight. Surprisingly, he felt no qualms at all when he saw it. He followed Ginger up the ramp, gazed down for a moment or two into the clear waters of the Mur, and then walked on unconcernedly past the guardhouse on the far bank of the river, past lounging off-duty Wehrmacht troops, who glanced at him indifferently, and continued up the road to the right. He was in Yugoslavia now, but he didn't cheer. He was still within the boundary of the Greater German Reich and within earshot and rifleshot of German guards, and the going might yet prove tricky.

There was no challenge. The two prisoners walked on, rounded a bend of the road, and came immediately to a huge building dug into the hillside, which Natusch guessed correctly was the Count's wine-cellar. Ginger stopped, and as he did, a youth in a grey huntsman's jacket got up from the side of the road and marched away at a brisk pace. The Count's plan was working. Natusch winked at Ginger as he passed the handcart, got an acknowledging thumbs-up from him by way of adieu, and carried on after the young man.

The youth set a far harder task than the New Zealander

had bargained for. One would have thought that the whole Wehrmacht were on the heels of that young Yugoslav. Natusch increased his pace and managed to keep up with him on the flat, but whenever they reached a hill, and there were several hills, he had to pull out all his reserves merely to keep his new guide in sight. His leg was still weak, and by the time they reached the third incline, he was lathered in sweat from pain and exertion, and begrimed with the dust of a long military convoy which had passed. He was beginning to doubt whether he'd be able to go on at all, but the youth was relentless. Possibly the sight of the Wehrmacht convoy with its tanks and half-tracks and four-barrelled A.A. guns had unnerved him: whether or not, he strode on at full speed, with never a glance behind until they cleared the populated area near the river and were once again in open country.

Natusch was on the verge of dropping back in despair when this racehorse of a Slav turned off the road and disappeared along a track by the side of a stream. The New Zealander got there a minute or two later, galloped along the track and almost stumbled over his elusive escort. The youth was kneeling in the long grass examining a bicycle. With him was a girl of about nineteen, a buxom wench with blue eyes and blonde hair, who turned and stared solicitously: and even then, exhausted as he was, and panting like a steam engine, Natusch couldn't fail but notice how very attractive this girl was. He gasped 'Hello' for want of brains and a better opening gambit, and straightaway flopped on the ground. He was dead beat.

The girl came over. 'How are you?' she asked. She spoke slowly, in English. 'Yuri is sorry he had to walk so fast, but he was told the Germans might follow you. How is your leg?'

Natusch lied bravely. 'It's fine,' he replied. 'First class. No trouble at all. Please thank Yuri for me.'

The girl's black dress, with its touch of lace at the collar, suited her perfectly, he reflected. He wasn't given opportunity to meditate further. A boy appeared on the track, wheeling another bicycle, and a minute later, Yuri and he were back on the main road, cycling over the last stretch of their journey.

They covered more than ten miles. Considerably more. The sun was going down when Yuri, a few yards in front, turned off the minor road they were now following, and pedalled along a path which ended abruptly at the edge of a wood. A tall man appeared from nowhere, grasped Natusch's hand and made a passionate and entirely unintelligible speech. 'He says he is glad to see you,' Yuri translated. It was the first time that the young man had spoken. He grinned. 'His name is Dusan and he doesn't like Germans. He is political. I will leave you now. Good luck.'

It was still 12th September, 1944. The date riveted itself in Natusch's memory, but later, he found that he could recall little of what happened to him and Dusan during the next two or three days. They had to cross the Windische Buheln, a hilly region between the Mur and the Drava River, where German patrols were active, and by day they slept in barns and outhouses and were fed by peasants who kept watch for them. The nights brought endless hours along rough tracks that meandered through the hills as they travelled west to Marburg, where a Partisan unit was waiting to send a convoy of recruits and escaped prisoners south to Tito.

The New Zealander said goodbye to Dusan in the hills east of Marburg on the night of 15th September. He was handed over to two soldiers, one dressed in Wehrmacht uniform, and the other in nondescript clothes that seemed to be of Italian origin. Both men were armed with automatic pistols, and wore the red star of Tito on their caps. They led their charge to a rendezvous above a small village, said something to a sergeant who came to meet them, grinned cheerfully at Natusch because neither side could understand a word the other said, and then vanished as noiselessly as they had appeared.

The sergeant and Natusch tried four languages before they hit on a common medium. 'Siete Inglese?' the Yugoslav asked eventually. He was a small man with a fierce moustache that bristled as he spoke.

Natusch watched it in fascination. 'No,' he replied, also in Italian. 'Not English. I'm a New Zealander.'

The sergeant grunted. It was a minor matter. 'Non fa niente,' he growled. 'You are a soldier?' That point wasn't argued, and the mobile moustache signified approval. 'Good!' the sergeant allowed. He eyed Natusch appraisingly, decided to trust him, and began biting off staccato remarks. 'I have here twelve recruits,' he announced. 'There are more farther south. We will join them. We march tonight and every night. By day we hide. You will keep watch for Germans, and you will stay near me. If we have to, we will fight. I will need you. I am Krivac. Sergeant Krivac.' His tone grew suddenly fierce. 'Ora, sono il vostro Duce. Capito?' The rising inflection of his voice, coupled with the prodigious authority of the moustache, jerked an answer from the New Zealander.

'Si, signor,' he agreed hastily. His hand shot up involuntarily in salute. 'Ho capito.'

Natusch kept on the fiery little sergeant's heels for the next five nights. He was given a battered Lee-Enfield rifle and a half a dozen clips of ammunition, which made the going heavier for him. As it happened, the little group didn't have to fight, which was perhaps as well. They maintained a keen watch for enemy patrols and saw two. On the second occasion, a score of Huns carrying automatic weapons passed in Indian file a hundred yards from the hidden fugitives. It was full daylight, and the shock left most of them pale and sweating.

But shocks and scares didn't stop the long night marches that were now taking a heavy toll of Natusch's weak leg. The Partisan sergeant, like all his colleagues, had a schedule to maintain, and with him, it was a case of best foot forward from dusk to dawn, and devil take the hindmost. He made no allowance for injuries and he would have abandoned Natusch, or anyone else, if they had fallen behind. But there wasn't any falling behind. Somehow, part of the time with his teeth gritted, Natusch kept accurate station two or three yards behind the wiry Yugoslav, watching him lest he should give a signal, watching the ground lest he should trip, cursing the Lee-Enfield for its increasing weight, and managing to keep a weather eye open for Germans as well.

The mood was infectious. None of the dozen men who were marching in the column failed to blaspheme the moustachioed brigand at the head of it regularly and fluently, but his very ruthlessness encouraged them to keep going, if only to thwart him. No one dropped out; and eventually, high up in the Posruk Hills on 22nd September, 1944, they reached the main band of recruits.

Natusch learnt from Sergeant Krivac, who was now relaxing slightly, that the new gathering numbered 150 men. That didn't surprise him, but the sergeant's 'Anche cento soldati' brought his eyebrows sharply to full lift. An escort, one hundred strong, the sergeant had said, was in the vicinity. That *was* large. Unusually so for a journey like this, but the Partisan chiefs knew what they were doing.

At sunset, the now silent convoy began moving through the forest on the long descent to the Drava River, and somewhere around midnight reached a village a mile or so above the crossing. Here they halted. There was danger here. Below them in a forest-clad gorge was a small ferry spanning this river that marked the frontier of the Greater Reich. The guards knew it as the only crossing place for miles around, and better perhaps, as a perilous place that was flanked by road and rail and open to sudden ambush by the Germans. The augmented escort remained on its toes, but this time, fortunately, there were no interruptions. The whole convoy, guards and all, crossed safely and vanished into the night: but for the space of two hours German-uniformed Partisans kept machine-guns peering grimly towards both ends of the gorge, whilst scouts armed with grenades and tommy-guns patrolled far beyond along both road and rail.

They maintained top speed and top vigil all night long. The guards, aware that this present country was a German stamping ground, set a pace that made Natusch and the others gasp and which took them past the danger spot of St. Lorenzen before dawn. A battalion of German infantry which had seen action against the Partisans, and which had been mauled, was stationed at St. Lorenzen. They gave the Wehrmacht a wide berth, rested during the day, reached the comparative safety of the Bacher Hills the next night, and there linked up with yet another 250 civilian recruits under the control of a Partisan officer. Among them were fifteen British soldiers who had recently escaped from a working camp near the border.

Lieutenant Cetinje, the Yugoslav officer, made a short speech. He was, he announced through his interpreter, in charge of the biggest convoy that had yet attempted to run the Nazi gauntlet south to Seisenberg. What was more, he intended to reach Seisenberg no matter what the Germans might put up against him. The fugitives could march where they pleased so long as they stayed with the convoy: and if any of his men had weapons to spare, those who preferred to be armed could take them and welcome.

As regards the order of march, the lieutenant added, getting down to detail, he was sending three scouts well ahead of the convoy to spy out the land. Behind them would march the main body of armed defenders, then the long column of civilians – overlong, Natusch thought – who would be flanked by roving escorts, and finally, a rearguard, heavily armed and with a fire-power that would make up for their lack of numbers. With that, the lieutenant stopped speaking, but his strategy was already clear to those who could appreciate it. Thus deployed, the vulnerable front and rear of the column would be protected, and so long as the unwieldy middle section didn't buckle, there seemed a sporting chance of being able to blast a way through any enemy opposition which might be met.

CHAPTER FOURTEEN

AMBUSH

THE Germans withheld their main attack for almost two weeks. Perhaps they didn't realize how frail the Partisan column was and what a plum was being offered them, and possibly the mauling that the St. Lorenzen garrison had taken made them over-cautious; but they *did* know that a column of Yugoslav guerrillas was travelling south through what they still regarded as their territory. Basic information like that was easily obtained. They guessed that they would be making for Seisenberg, a hundred miles farther to the south, where the German fiat expired and where Tito's rule began; but their initial reaction was half-hearted. The Wehrmacht were fewer in number than they had been, and their Intelligence was poorly served.

During the week that followed, they sent out patrols who exacted a toll of the civilians and fought bloody and ferocious skirmishes with the Partisan soldiery and their British allies, but there weren't enough patrols to stop the convoy. The Germans no longer had men in plenty. Their best units had long since left for the Eastern Front, and their fighting vehicles were unable to deploy to advantage in this savage wooded countryside. Victory of a kind was theirs, nevertheless. Overworked Partisan scouts were forced to lead their charges off route into districts where the going was hard, and where sometimes they had to march all day without a bite to eat. Privation weakened them, continual alarms sapped their nervous energy, and these twin hazards soon began to exact as big a toll as the German sharpshooters.

Some of the civilians, unable to maintain the unrelenting pace which Lieutenant Cetinje set, dropped out of the column and were left behind. Their numbers increased as enemy pressure kept the marchers away from hidden food dumps and as iron rations grew smaller: nor could the scattered villages and hamlets they passed through hope to feed over four hundred people. 'Na zalost – nimamo nicesar' ('Sorry – we have nothing') was repeated all too often, and still more exhausted Yugoslavs dropped out as this fresh privation proved too much.

It didn't discourage Sergeant Krivac. He seemed to be made of wire and muscle, and Natusch, still following faithfully behind him, began to wonder if the irascible sergeant's stamina knew any limit. By now, the New Zealander's respect for the little Yugoslav martinet, particularly during the more sustained of the Wehrmacht attacks, had grown almost to the point of devotion. Krivac, he acknowledged unstintingly, was the complete guerrilla.

The convoy trudged on. Bedraggled, often weary beyond belief, and for the most part in cold rainy weather, they made their way south over the mountains behind the Fiestritz valley to Partisan-held Cilli, and arrived there in early October. They were well fed that day. They ate and slept and managed to restore some of their physical and nervous energy, but the next morning brought everyone sharply back to normal. By ten o'clock, the convoy was once again on the road.

The reason was simple. There was no 'front' in the accepted sense in this struggle between Partisans and Germans, and whole areas were dominated first by one side and then the other. The control of Cilli, it appeared, was a knife-edged affair, and the Partisan officers there had no intention of being hampered by a large body of what were virtually non-combatants. They sent Lieutenant Cetinje and his cohort brusquely on their way with what provisions they could spare, and added a warning that the fifteen miles to Mottnig, the next stopping place, were not yet free from enemy attack. The way led through ideal ambushing country which imposed an almost superhuman alert on the escorts, but the Germans missed an easy target.

Lieutenant Cetinje could allow his weary band only a brief few hours' rest at Mottnig. It was another disputed zone, another Cilli, and as dusk gathered they set off once again on an overnight march to the Partisan stronghold of Littai. Beyond Littai, as everyone knew, lay the last lap of this ferocious journey. Sixteen miles farther south was Seisenberg – and freedom. There were no German forces behind the line of the Gurk River.

The convoy pushed on through the night at top speed, but by now almost everyone was weary and overmarched, and towards dawn the tight schedule collapsed. First light found them still over four miles from the haven of Littai – and vulnerable. German forces, they had been told, were in this area, too.

The first birds were making experimental *cheep-cheeps* as the convoy emerged from their belt of forest which had so far concealed it. Ahead of them was a road, wide, empty, almost ruler-straight – and devoid of cover. It vanished behind a vaporish mist even as they watched.

Natusch noticed that the Partisan soldiers were carrying their weapons at the ready. He checked the German rifle which had replaced his battered Lee-Enfield, gestured to Sergeant Krivac at his side, and thumbed back the safety catch.

He heard nothing as they marched on. No one heard anything, or saw anything, until a gust of wind momentarily lifted the enveloping mist. Natusch halted instantly, his outstretched arm barring the way to Sergeant Krivac. The vanguard of the convoy were on the point of entering a natural depression. All around them the ground rose gently, like the rim of a saucer, to woods on either side and to what appeared to be vineyards on the skyline eighty yards away. It was an ideal place for a trap; a perfect setting undoubtedly, for the command 'Feuer!' that bit sharp and incisive, and a shade premature, through the morning air.

Natusch hurled himself to the ground as machine-guns in the vineyards opened up. Behind him, two men staggered and fell. One of them dropped by his side, coughed, spewed a red froth of blood over the New Zealander's arm and gave a sudden violent 'Oh!' as another bullet hit his prone body. The ambushers were aiming low, raking the ground with their fire, seeking out those who had taken cover.

Natusch could see no future in staying put. He jumped up and sprinted through some bushes towards the shelter of the forest, others following him as still more clods of earth leapt upwards. A stream of tracer pursued them and they dived as one man for the slim sanctuary of the furrows as it streaked past. Explosive bullets joined the tracer and began thudding into the ground, showering soft earth on some, taking their lethal toll of others.

Natusch ran and then dived again to escape the lash of close-flying bullets. They missed him, but a burst caught Harry Childs, one of the Englishmen who was running behind him. Childs died instantly. It was only then that Natusch realized that he was unarmed, that he had nothing to hit back with. The bushes he had raced through had torn the rifle from his grasp.

The Germans had set their trap expertly. Littai was held by the Partisans, but the surrounding countryside was theirs, and their Intelligence was at last functioning. They had waylaid the convoy all too successfully; and they had killed Harry Childs. A sudden rage seized Natusch. He got up, ran back a few yards to where Childs had fallen, and grabbed the Lee-Enfield which lay beside his dead comrade. He gave the weapon a lightning check and flattened himself hard into the ground behind a small ridge.

The mist which once again had concealed the action lifted momentarily. Natusch scanned the vineyard ahead over the sights of the rifle, and saw nothing. There were no Germans visible, no machine-gun nest, no snipers, nothing except the black stumps of the vines, some of them hidden by clusters of still ungathered grapes. He checked again carefully, meticulously, freezing the vineyard a section at a time from behind the Lee-Enfield. There was still nothing. He blinked hard as the returning mist danced along the slope, and suddenly detected a tiny movement at the extreme edge of the field. He pinpointed the spot, his rage now gone entirely, and squeezed the trigger. An answering shriek came as his second bullet homed in the merest shade to the left of the first. He fired five times into the tight arc of the camouflaged enemy position, the shots masked and anonymous in the renewed hubbub of battle. There was no reply.

He reached the forest alone. The men who had fled with him had vanished, and Natusch realized quite suddenly that he had lost Sergeant Krivac. He looked around anxiously, but there was no sign of the wiry Yugoslav, nor indeed of anyone else. The all-concealing mist was once again obliterating the battlefield. A sudden wave of fatigue came, and he slumped down behind a tree to rest briefly and to collect his thoughts.

He got up again as the Wehrmacht attack entered its second phase and mortar crews began arching shells into the wood. He moved quickly from the noise of the bursts, and almost immediately stumbled across a group of men sheltering behind some trees. None was armed. They looked up in alarm as Natusch approached, recognized him, and at that moment the high bang of a mortar shell sounded from a copse nearby. Everyone dropped flat. The recruits were shaken, some terror-stricken, but they recovered fast and obeyed Natusch's gesture as he led them to safer ground.

The New Zealander knew then that he would have to stay with these men. He had no option. If any Germans were to venture into the wood, he might or might not be able to hold them, but without his slender protection these Yugoslavs would be as sheep to the slaughter. He pushed a fresh clip into the magazine of the Lee-Enfield, dispersed the huddled group, and took up a position behind a tree. Dense undergrowth concealed him. A thought occurred as he adjusted the sights of the rifle. If the Germans did come, it would be a fight to the finish. It would have to be. If he were to be recaptured the Gestapo would be unlikely to botch a third chance of interrogating their much-wanted Captain Natusch of Szigetvar.

Natusch went on speculating, trying now to piece together the jigsaw of this present encounter. The bulk of the convoy and certainly most of the armed escort, he decided, must be in the larger wood on the other side of the road. He hadn't seen anyone other than his own band of frightened men. The Wehrmacht were having it all their own way, too, largely because of their skilful positioning, but their strategy wasn't as good as it had seemed earlier on. They hadn't placed hidden snipers in the wood, far less machine-guns, and they hadn't waited until the convoy was squarely in their sights. Another thirty seconds would have made all the difference. Natusch grinned despite himself. Van Clausewitz wouldn't have given them high marks for this exercise.

A sudden upsurge of violence cut short his meditation. The battle veered away from the hidden recruits and their lone protector as a rain of shells began falling on the wood opposite. The Wehrmacht, secure in their ambush position on higher ground, had guessed where their enemy was concealed. Natusch heard distant cries and shrieks, and then above the continuing explosions, the rattle of machine-gun fire as the Partisan soldiery began to outflank the Germans. He lay prone, his weapon at the ready, alert for the Wehrmacht scouts whom he knew could be sent out.

He saw no one. The forest on his side of the road remained still, and abruptly his thoughts turned to Sergeant Krivac again. Where was Krivac, he wondered? Was he all right? Somehow it seemed impossible to imagine otherwise. Krivac, of all people, was a born survivor. Natusch wished fervently that the quick-tempered Yugoslav was with him now. Krivac would know what to do here far better than he, would be a pillar of strength.

The battle continued. It went on for the better part of another half-hour, with incessant mortaring and small-arms fire, all of it veering still farther away from the road, when suddenly the noise of heavier weapons sounded, and for a moment Natusch thought that he recognized the hiss of flame-throwers. A faint cheering reached him as the tumult erupted into a crescendo. Partisan reinforcements from Littai had arrived at last to engage the Germans and to save what was left of their ill-fated convoy.

The third and final phase of the engagement was short-lived. Heavy exchanges of gunfire continued for a while, but gradually the uproar subsided until at length it was replaced by almost total silence. Natusch stayed hidden. It was clear now that the Germans were too few in numbers to have risked a frontal assault along the road, or to slog it out with the Littai Partisans, but they might well choose to retreat through his part of the wood. He remained where he was for perhaps another fifteen minutes, watching and waiting, before finally getting up and signalling the relieved band of recruits to follow him.

He regained the road to find that the battle really had finished. Heavily armed guerrillas were standing on guard, very much on the alert, whilst their Red Cross men brought out the wounded and placed them gently at the verge. Some of them were desperately hurt. Natusch recognized one of the ex-prisoners standing nearby, and approached him. Yes, the Englishman said, casualties were heavy. Best part of a hundred killed. A lot wounded, too. Those first mortar shells had landed smack in the middle of the recruits. Blew God knows how many to bits. Milling about in the wood, they were, instead of getting their heads down.

There was a pause before Natusch pressed his further question. Yes, the infantryman answered again. He looked surprised. Of course he knew Sergeant Krivac. Everyone knew him. Fierce little fellow with no nerves. Hell of a fighter, too. No, he regretted he hadn't seen him.

Natusch felt his alarm escalating as he left the road and entered the wood which had witnessed so much ferocity and slaughter. He was trying unsuccessfully to convince himself. Not Krivac, he argued. The Jerries couldn't kill Krivac. Nobody could. The unsuspected strength of their bond and friendship began to dawn on him. He walked on, avoided stumbling over the dead and parts of the dead, reflecting as he had done on previous occasions that heavy mortar bombs make clumsy killlers, and turned over a dozen men in his search for the little Yugoslav martinet. He didn't find him. Hope came, a sudden buoyant awareness that Krivac was too experienced to be caught in a massacre like this, that he would be laughing at his fears, and hope blossomed instantly into certainty. It left Natusch wholly unprepared for the final blow that the war was to deal him.

He was turning away from the shambles which confronted him when he froze, stiffened in sudden horror. A little apart from the mass of dead men, and somehow neat and precise in the midst of all this carnage, was Sergeant Krivac. The peppery Yugoslav gazed sternly at Natusch through one eye, unblinking and uncompromising as ever, the prodigious authority of his moustache undiminished despite the rivulet of blood which threatened to bedraggle it. His other eye and the greater part of his forehead had been scythed away by the mortar fragment.

An augmented escort and what was left of the convoy reached Littai a few hours later. They saw none of the Wehrmacht troops who had lain in ambush against them, other than their dead and badly wounded. The Germans had suffered too, had been hit hard by the Partisans.

Natusch marched near the front of the depleted column, a Schmeisser automatic replacing the Lee-Enfield, alert for further ambush, and with his mind now closed against the pain and shock of Sergeant Krivac's death. They met no one. Three days later, the convoy, bearing their wounded in lorries and horsedrawn carts, crossed the Gurk River into Seisenberg. They weren't molested on this journey either, which was as well. The toll which had been exacted of them was the heaviest that the Partisan guerrillas had yet sustained. Of the original 500-odd who had set out in high spirits from the Posruk Hills just over a month ago, less than 300 were still on their feet.

Natusch left the stronghold of Seisenberg next day for the last part of his long journey. He travelled alone, no longer armed, and walked in driving rain to Toplitz, and from there south to the larger town of Mottling. The travel documents and pass which the Seisenberg commander gave him eased the passage. On 19th October, 1944, he entered Tschernombl, passed some white, battle-scarred buildings by a German-destroyed concrete bridge that had once spanned the Kulpa River, and walked another twelve miles to a village called Semic. Three miles farther on, he had been told, was an airstrip used by transport planes which brought in munitions from Italy.

He waited at Semic for a whole week. Not a single aircraft came near the place during this time, but alarming reports filtered through to the effect that German Stuka pilots had been told about the airstrip, and had it on their visiting list. It was a dull week, and rained constantly except for the last day, when ten survivors of the British contingent of the convoy arrived from Seisenberg. Their five colleagues, they said simply and without elaboration, were missing.

The evening of 28th October saw eleven men assembled at the airstrip. Two planes were due that night, a Whitley bomber and an American aircraft; and for no reason at all, Natusch's instinct began warning him that all was far from well. Nor was it mistaken. They found a number of Partisan soldiers waiting to light petrol-soaked signal fires; and they discovered too that the heavy rains of the last few days had left a wide sheet of water down the middle of the runway. It was more a lake than a landing ground.

The Whitley pilot agreed. They picked up the faint drone of his engines at half past nine, put a light to the fires, and waited apprehensively as he circled overhead. He went round several times. Natusch thought he was putting his flaps down to land, and his heart jumped, but he should have known better. A message that was brief and unsympathetic flashed out from the plane. Couldn't be done, the pilot signalled. He was sorry, but if he were to land in that puddle he'd likely break the plane. And his neck. Better go back rather than risk a pile-up. It was an obvious decision, and reluctantly those on the ground had to agree with it.

Half an hour later, the American pilot arrived. He circled the airstrip twice, endorsed his colleague's decision, and as the sound of his engines died away, hope died with them. A brisk patter of raindrops suddenly fell on the airstrip. They pricked the surface water of the runway in a thousand places, hissed on the now dying signal fires, and breathed a warning of the approaching storm.

One of the Englishmen turned up the collar of his coat. They might as well go back to the farmhouse as stay where they were, he suggested, because there would be no more planes that night, and there was no sense in getting soaked to the skin. Natusch was the only one to disagree. He did so because the Partisans in charge of the petrol fires had told him that a Russian plane was also coming, and that it was to collect the dozen wounded men who were lying in bullock carts nearby waiting for it. He pointed this out to the others, stressed that the plane was a Balkan Airforce transport *en route* to Bari, and that there'd likely be room for everyone, but no one seemed to have any faith in the report. Some wag was asking whether the Russky would use wheels or floats when a sudden deluge put an end to banter. Quite suddenly, Natusch was the sole Briton at the airstrip.

The two hours until midnight didn't tax him overmuch. He was used to waiting, and the Partisans had no doubt at all but that the aircraft would arrive. They kept their ears open for it, tried to shelter in the lee of the covered bullock carts, and chattered away in German to Natusch with a zest that decreased as time went by. Zest vanished altogether about half an hour after midnight. From then on, the only sounds that were heard were the nagging patter of raindrops and occasional groans from the more seriously wounded Partisans.

Natusch stood, leaning against one of the carts, soaked to

the skin, wondering if the Russian really did intend to fly in. He hoped hard that he would. He would have to, he reflected grimly, if the wounded Partisans were to have any chance at all. No further planes were due for another nine days, which meant that they might as well write off the airstrip. If the rains didn't destroy it, it was hardly likely that the Stuka pilots would fail as well. There were, too, those uncomplaining wounded Partisan soldiers. Natusch looked in helpless sympathy at the line of bullock carts. The men in them lay on their crude stretchers, hurt, pathetic, calling dumbly for aid and a little comfort, and swaying the issue not at all. There are always wounded in time of war: their lot is always a hard one.

It was well past one o'clock before they heard the Russky. By then, hope had become a very faint spark indeed, but it flared up with the same frenzy as the newly drenched petrol fires. The noise grew quickly, and they stared upwards at the plane as it roared low overhead. Signal lights flashed and were returned. It was the Russian, late but not too late. Heavy rain splashed on the flooded airstrip as he circled and roared overhead again, examining the sheet of water below. He vanished into the darkness, banked, and came back a third time as great gouts of flame from the signal fires seared the air. The Partisans were throwing on petrol recklessly, willing the Russian to land.

It was as if he understood. He banked once again and this time cut his motors as he approached the airstrip. Landing lights shone out. The pilot gunned his engines momentarily, then cut them right back, and they watched fascinated as his landing lights sank rapidly to the ground. The plane bounced gently as it touched down and rushed towards the flooded part of the runway. A confused cacophony sounded as the heavy machine entered the miniature lake and spray thundered on its underside. It vanished in what seemed to be a great wall of water, and then it was through and was turning towards them, still in one piece, its pilot waving to them, its motors rumbling loud above the cheering of the Partisans.

The plane left again in a matter of minutes. It took that long to unload the weapons and ammunition it was carrying and to place the wounded aboard. Natusch jumped in, waved to the Partisan soldiers and lost sight of them immediately as the fuselage doors swung to. The engines were roaring impatiently. Their noise increased as the plane once again charged the water, shook off its grip and came dangerously near the extremity of the runway before lumbering slowly, almost reluctantly, into the air. It gained height, circled the airstrip once, and then set off on the long haul to Bari in southern Italy.

Natusch sat on the bare metal floor of the Russian aircraft. He was tired. Dog-tired. It had been a long day. He shook his head, trying to dispel the fatigue, and saw one of the wounded soldiers watching him compassionately. 'Schlafen,' the Yugoslav advised gently. He placed his sound hand to his cheek explanatorily. 'Morgenfruh,' he went on, in the enemy tongue that was their only link. 'Morgenfruh, nicht Deutsch, nicht Gestapo, nur Englisch.' He smiled. 'Ist gut. Ja?'

THE END

FIVE ROADS TO FREEDOM BY GEORGE BEESON

'If you can't dig your way out, kid your way out and if that fails think again . . .'

George Beeson was a genius among escapers in the Second World War. A Sergeant in the R.A.S.C., he was captured and taken prisoner in 1940. After a gruelling forced-march into Poland, without medical aid (he had been wounded) and with the absolute minimum of barely edible food, he arrived at Poznan P.O.W. camp. From there on, he occupied himself with escaping. In all he made five separate attempts and finally got away.

With modesty and humour, the author describes the horrors of the eastern camps, the long battle of wits with his later captors and his extraordinary adventures with the French Resistance. The result is an enthralling and deeply moving book.

0 552 10714 X 70p

GREEN BEACH BY JAMES LEASOR

One man – one mission . . . and one of the greatest true stories of courage during World War II.

On the 19th August 1942 six thousand Canadian and British commandos strike at Hitler's Europe. With them is one young man – a man whose mission is so vital that he cannot possibly be allowed to fall into enemy hands . . . alive.

'GREEN BEACH has blown the lid off one of the Second World War's best-kept secrets'. – The Daily Express.

0 552 10245 8 75p

A SELECTED LIST OF WAR BOOKS PUBLISHED BY CORGI

WHILE EVERY EFFORT IS MADE TO KEEP PRICES LOW, IT IS SOMETIMES NECESSARY TO INCREASE PRICES AT SHORT NOTICE. CORGI BOOKS RESERVE THE RIGHT TO SHOW AND CHARGE NEW RETAIL PRICES ON COVERS WHICH MAY DIFFER FROM THOSE ADVERTISED IN THE TEXT OR ELSEWHERE.

THE PRICES SHOWN BELOW WERE CORRECT AT THE TIME OF GOING TO PRESS (MAY' 78)

	Number	Title	Author	Price
☐	09929 5	**The Last Dogfight**	*Martin Caldin*	60p
☐	10400 0	**The Bloody Road to Death**	*Sven Hassel*	85p
☐	09761 6	**Blitzfreeze**	*Sven Hassel*	85p
☐	09178 2	**Reign of Hell**	*Sven Hassel*	95p
☐	08874 9	**SS General**	*Sven Hassel*	85p
☐	08779 3	**Assignment Gestapo**	*Sven Hassel*	95p
☐	08603 7	**Liquidate Paris**	*Sven Hassel*	85p
☐	08528 6	**March Battalion**	*Sven Hassel*	75p
☐	08168 X	**Monte Cassino**	*Sven Hassel*	85p
☐	07871 9	**Comrades of War**	*Sven Hassel*	85p
☐	07242 7	**Wheels of Terror**	*Sven Hassel*	85p
☐	07241 9	**Legion of the Damned**	*Sven Hassel*	85p
☐	10080 3	**The First 100,000**	*Ian Hay*	60p
☐	10343 8	**Cross of Iron**	*Willi Heinrich*	75p
☐	09485 4	**The Savage Mountain**	*Willi Heinrich*	65p
☐	10393 4	**The Blue Max**	*Jack D. Hunter*	75p
☐	08371 2	**The Dirty Dozen**	*E. M. Nathanson*	£1.00
☐	10035 8	**The Beardless Warriors**	*Richard Matheson*	50p
☐	09932 5	**Private Navy**	*David Satherley*	50p
☐	10057 9	**The Deathmakers**	*Glen Sire*	65p
☐	10155 9	**633 Squadron: Operation Rhine Maiden**	*Frederick E. Smith*	75p
☐	08169 8	**633 Squadron**	*Frederick E. Smith*	65p
☐	10273 3	**The Giant Killers**	*John Oram Thomas*	85p
☐	09874 4	**Hunters from the Sky**	*Charles Whiting*	50p
☐	10454 X	**Tank**	*David Williams*	75p

All these books are available at your bookshop or newsagent, or can be ordered direct from the publisher. Just tick the titles you want and fill in the form below.

CORGI BOOKS, Cash Sales Department, P.O. Box 11, Falmouth, Cornwall.

Please send cheque or postal order, no currency.

U.K. send 22p for first book plus 10p per copy for each additional book ordered to a maximum charge of 82p to cover the cost of postage and packing.

B.F.P.O. and Eire allow 22p for first book plus 10p per copy for the next 6 books, thereafter 4p per book.

Overseas Customers. Please allow 30p for the first book and 10p per copy for each additional book.

NAME (Block letters)..

ADDRESS ....

....